On a Wing of the Sun

For Sage
with all best wishes—
Jim
9/27/10
Santa Fe

On a Wing of the Sun

Three Volumes of Poetry
by Jim Barnes

[signature: Jim Barnes]

University of Illinois Press
Urbana and Chicago

© 2001 by Jim Barnes
All rights reserved
Manufactured in the United States of America
1 2 3 4 5 C P 5 4 3 2 1

The American Book of the Dead (1982) was first published by the
University of Illinois Press. The poems from *A Season of Loss* (1985)
and *La Plata Cantata* (1989) are used by arrangement with the original
publisher, Purdue University Press, and may not be reprinted elsewhere
without authorization.

∞ This book is printed on acid-free paper.

Library of Congress Cataloging-in-Publication Data
Barnes, Jim, 1933–
On a wing of the sun : three volumes of poetry / by Jim Barnes.
  p.   cm.
ISBN 0-252-02704-3 (acid-free paper)
ISBN 0-252-07015-1 (pbk. : acid-free paper)
I. Title.
PS3552.A67395A6   2001
811'.54—dc21   2001002243

The hawk sweeps in on a wing of the sun,
breaks to a stop, trembling and still,
like a skater at the perilous edge of ice
breathing a silent strength.
 —"Domain"

CONTENTS

THE AMERICAN BOOK OF THE DEAD (1982)

The American Book of the Dead   2

1. This Crazy Land
    Autobiography, Chapter 1: Leaving Summerfield   4
    The Chicago Odyssey   5
    On the Beach at Manzanita, Oregon   6
    Autobiographical Flashback: Puma and Pokeweed   8
    Still-Hildreth Sanitarium: Fishing   9
    These Mysteries   10
    Last Look at La Plata, Missouri   12
    Return to La Plata, Missouri   13
    An Ex–Deputy Sheriff Remembers the Eastern Oklahoma Murderers   14
    Autobiography, Chapter 7: Home for Memorial Day   18

2. Death by Water
    Sundown at Swan Lake, Missouri   20
    The Body Falters   22
    On the Eve of My Parents' Sixtieth Anniversary   24
    Old Soldiers' Home at Marshalltown, Iowa   25
    Swan Lake, Again   26
    Pyramid Lake, Late Summer   28
    For a Drowned Sailor, Age 4   29
    Elegy for the Girl Who Drowned at Goats Bluff   30
    Postcard to Grace Schulman   31
    Autobiography, Chapter 17: Floating the Big Piney   32
    Scouting Tom Fry Hollow   33
    On Top of Winding Stair Mountain   34
    Under Buffalo Mountain   35

Autobiography, Chapter 14: Tombstone at Petit Bay, near Tahlequah 36
Still-Hildreth Sanitarium: Ice Fishing 37
Autobiography, Chapter 6: San Diego Harbor at Dusk 38
Tracking the Siuslaw Man 39
San Miguel de Allende 40
The Last Trip Somewhere West 41
Autobiography, Chapter 16: Return to Rich Mountain 42
Comcomly's Skull 43
Autobiography, Chapter 15: Agate Beach, California 44
The Only Photograph of Quentin at Harvard 45

3. Ishmael

My Father's House 48
Origin 50
The Good Dark 51
Tonight the Moon 52
Autobiography, Chapter 13: Ghost Train, the Dream 53
After Dreams 54
The Ghost's Story 55
After a Postcard from Stryk in Japan 56
Autobiography, Chapter 12: Hearing Montana 57
In Rudolph's Cave 58
Autobiography, Chapter 3: Nearing El Paso 59
Dog Days 1978 60
One for Grand Ronde, Oregon 61
Autobiography, Chapter 18: Camp in the Dead of Summer 62
Lost in Sulphur Canyons 64
Autobiography, Chapter 9: Leaving, Again 66
The Iowa Sequence 67
Autobiography, Chapter 11: Prelude to Writing 70
Memoirs of a Catskinner 72
On the Bridge at Fourche Maline River 74
The Last Chance 75

4. Night Falls, Ritual and Fast
    Year's End 1977   78
    Winter Pastoral   79
    Contemporary Native American Poetry   80
    Midwest Midwinter   81
    Autobiography, Chapter 2: Setting Out   83
    The Exact Center of the World   84
    Against Metempsychosis &c.   85
    Autobiography, Chapter 19: For Andrew Grossbardt, in Memoriam   87
    Autobiography, Chapter 4: The Mirage   88
    Wild Horse Hollow   89
    Autobiography, Chapter 5: Ghost Town   90
    Autobiography, Chapter 8: At the Sand Fields   91
    Loving the Distant Nude   92
    The Family Plot   93
    Tornado   94
    Stopping on Kiamichi Mountain   95
    Autobiography, Chapter 42: Three Days in Louisville   97
    Self-Portrait   100
    Autobiography: Last Chapter   101

A SEASON OF LOSS (1985)

1. Bone Yard
    Bone Yard   106
    Paiute Ponies   107
    La Plata, Missouri: Clear November Night   108
    Halcyon Days   109
    Near Crater Lake   110
    Thunderstorm in a Nevada Ghost Town   111
    A Rannaigheacht Ghairid on Spring Burning   112
    Song of I-see-o   113
    In Memory of a Day Nobody Remembers: September 26, 1874   114

January Wind 115
At the Burn on the Oregon Coast 116
On the Mountain 117
Right Place, Wrong Time 118
Postcard from Poison Spider Creek, Wyoming 119
Trying to Hide Out on Rich Mountain 120
Four Things Choctaw 121
Choctaw Cemetery 123
Rabbits 124
Black Mesa Sundown 125
Reading Santa Fe 126
Black Mesa Nocturn 128
Badlands Mirage 129
A Sunday Dreamer's Guide to Yarrow, Missouri 130
A Season of Loss 131
A Song for All of Them 132
A Season of Sun Dogs 133

2. Dog Days

Dog Days 136
Rest Stop at Horse Thief Spring 137
Sweating It Out on Winding Stair Mountain 138
Return to the Roundup Tavern 139
The Long Lone Nevada Night Highway 141
Dirge 142
Decades 144
Yuma: The Greyhound Depot 146
The Sentence 147
Notes for a Love Letter from Mid-America 148
Sundays 151
For Geoffrey Firmin, in Hell 152
Odyssey 154
Surviving the Storm 156
Autobiography, Chapter 10: Circus in the Blood 158

On Location at Tongue River   159
Crow   160
The Drowning   161
Heartland   163
Ghost Fog   164
The Captive Stone   165
Parable   166
Accident at Three Mile Island   167
Toy Soldiers   168
The Pawnbroker Takes Final Inventory   170
Call It Going with the Sun   172
5-Ring Circus at Season's End   174

LA PLATA CANTATA (1989)

Gill Netting the Beaver Pond   177
Surveying near Ellsworth, Kansas   180
The Heavener Runes   181
Near Cimarron, New Mexico   182
Great Plains Tornado   183
South Willamette Valley Bars: A Memoir   184
Circus Poster   186
Once in Winnemucca   187
Stations   188
Dreams the Children Had   190
Icons   191
Something in the Blood   194
Trying to Read the Glyphs   195
Postcard from Blue Finger Lake   196
Learning Balance   197
Going after the Milch Cow   198
Touching the Rattlesnake   199
Hunting Winding Stair Mountain   201
First Cavalry: Holson Valley Road, 1942   203

The War over Holson Valley   204
Bombardier   205
The Submarine in the Park between the Muskogee Toll Road and the Arkansas River   209
Memories of Oceanside   211
The Game   213
Ubi Sunt   214
Night Letter to the Secretary of the Interior   215
Domain   217
Paraglyphs   218
Three Songs from a Texas Oilfield   221
At 39: The View from Sycamore Tower   222
Below the Sans Bois Mountain   223
In Hugo Country   224
Horsefly, B.C.   225
Crossing the Kiamichis Again   226
La Plata Cantata   227
For the Suicide   238
Deer Camp: Blue Mountain   239
From the Swinging Bridge   240

Acknowledgments   241

The American Book of the Dead

The American Book of the Dead

To be rolled up the size of a small god's scroll,
to be placed in the journeyer's good right hand,
to be, as it were, an extra finger

                                        touching the stilled heart,
                                        requesting voice.

To have been written by a company of good poets,
to have been judged a map of the right way,
to have been perceived at the moment of passing

                                        by the voyager at the gate.

So that the words not ring hollow
down the corridors of doom or dome,

                                        let the last little book

be of softest vellum, only a whispering skin,
that may fade as the body fades

                                        before Eridanus or the Po.

Let us all carry into death the words we could not,
lifebound, bear and in whatever other worlds

                                        say them unafraid.

ONE

This Crazy Land

Henry lay in de netting, wild,
while the brainfever bird did scales;
Mr. Heartbreak, the New Man,
come to farm a crazy land;
an image of the dead on the fingernail
of a newborn child.
—John Berryman, "Dream Song 5"

Autobiography, Chapter 1: Leaving Summerfield

Low wind across old weeds warps your sense of hours;
    the day is heavy with cloud and slow hawks.

The last false-front you catch sight of cracks
    the color of old harness, rattles like bone
    chimes in a wind you know you will never
    see clear through.

The road straight out is black with tar oozed
    into itself; fenced against the road, the weeds
    wait out the wire.

The sun has danced upon this town and gone; not
    even a mirage is left to lie you lives you
    sometimes thought you'd live.

There's a distant sound of bells you know don't ring.

The last false-front is falling with your years;
    your eyes are webbing with the panes.

You curse the damned town for all you're worth,
    but know you'll have to come home again,
    fast as a rabid fox, when the years have made
    the town quick with old men's dream.

The Chicago Odyssey

Looking north you try to break through the sky
with your bad eyes. You want to map the town.
The lake and leaden sky are one, a blank
canvas on which you'd like to sketch a face.
The artist in you tells you to wait for dream.
You wait and nothing comes. You try museums,
their rigid worth, view mummies and other
wonders hardly half as strange as this place,
this time. A gauze of snow spirals up your spine.
You tell yourself the ice age now begins
and you alone must escape to tell the tale:
the horror of his and hers fleshed in frost,
the scream caught suddenly in mid-flight,
the running child quick-frozen in the park,
towers icicled in reverse, the el turned
easy slope for otters.

                All as the world turns
the other way. You turn and traffic whirs.
The astronomy is wrong: there are no stars,
moon breaks crystalline, the only zodiac
is flake on flake, a kaleidoscope of air.
You swore you'd know this town and now you don't.
Something has tipped the day and up is down;
you're trying your best to leave while there's still
a time. From each corner comes a siren's song.
Every street's a cliff you tack away from,
cotton in your ears against the damning wind
you never thought could be so cold, so insistent
on its icy trade, that barter would mean
the loss of teeth. You'll suck your eyes back in
your head, lean hard into the coming night,
lie always, go native, and by God survive.

On the Beach at Manzanita, Oregon

FOR TOM AND CHRIS, CHOCTAW AND YUCHI

Over my shoulder Neahkanie Mountain
parts the wind and clouds headed for Bend,
and here stands a stone marked by unknown hands:
two centuries' scribbling on this salt sea stone.
Clatsop, Spaniard, local loggers' marks?
Big Tree says his people used to dig up beeswax
by tons at Nehalem Spit to trade for glass
when the land was young and sea was hard for ships.
The cryptic stone faces seaward, its secret
kept: townsfolk say a hoard of gold lies buried
beneath the sand, just under the mountain's eye.
But buried is not the word:

                        Listen to the wind,
hear the dip of oars in waves the Clatsop braved
to look for smelt or beeswax on the beach,
remember the man who breathed salt air and spruce
who too once stood on this smooth plot of earth.

Time ebbs, ebbs for me as I stand beside
the hallowed stone and think of steelhead running
and Spanish bones down deep out there and sift
the black granite sand through my fingers here
while the ageless Chinook works its warm way through
the tunnels in my mind.

                    A dying race,
the Yuchis of Oklahoma can count but few
of their tribe alive. Drowned Phoenician sailors.
In our adopted land when Chief and I
were twelve or so, we rode the prairies west,
west and back again, bareback and double
astride the fast bay mare our fathers had.

Once we could not hold on and plunged headlong
into the rolling waves of wind on sage
while the bay coursed on across horizons red
with Yuchi paint.

    The sounds of sea strike deep
the chords of memory. The stone stands silent,
immense in its place on this northern strand.

Autobiographical Flashback: Puma and Pokeweed

I've spoken of home before and spotted crows
older than my hair. I generalize: home
is where hard is. And know it true. The crow
is constant color: his caw can crack a stone.

You keep your crows alive as best you can:
you remember a puma and pokeweed and trees
quick with wings and wind, tell yourself the fear
you felt along your fingertips would freeze

your sanity now, if you were child again,
free to feel again leaves upon your head,
to break off shoots of poke for suppertime,
to dream the cry of a puma one time heard.

Your memory is rocked by things you have
neglected; your stoned eyes are hard with world
you are late to see. And even now you know
the facts are wrong, as random and whorled

as fingerprints on records you've tried to keep
or the circling crows that blot your inland sky.

Still-Hildreth Sanitarium: Fishing

You come here when there's nothing else to do:
the kids in school, the wife working ten to
four, you off for months you don't care to count.
The sanitarium stands as empty as your head
must be to know the place in full. The flood
of bathing ghosts around the private lake
takes your mind, wave after wave, until you
drown in things you can never really know,
but think you can.

                The cracking skylight three
stories above your head is bound to fall
upon the ballroom floor where other ghosts
know no end to dance and music forever
spiels. You could go mad here except for needs.
The bass you plan to take from the darker side
of the lake were spawned when the grounds
were rich from insanity. But you are sane,
the water is sane, the day is sane.

                You know
this sanctuary Van Johnson chose to dry out in
is a marvel you can never reckon with.
Why it failed had something to do with dollars
and decay. Upkeep and appearance were
vital as the light it took for Van
to see the light. Windows crack under your
eyes. Even ghosts are drowning in current dance.
You fish for bass and contemplate the end.

These Mysteries

Walking these hills
you have a sense
of distance:

each stone
a mystery
in relation
to all others.

The space between
is question.

Then
the unnatural
shape
marks earth:

a sharp wonder.

Obsidian chipped
so perfect
the sky's a lie.

Hand and eye
you try
the black edges:

the minuscule contours
of hill, hollow,
the semblance
of a dead sea.

A ghost
in your bones
begins a dance,
a rhythm of blood
you cannot name.

These hills
where the hawk
is silent,

these hills
where the crow
has forgotten the caw,

these hills,
these mysteries,
cloud your eyes
as earth
the agate.

You want to know
the secret of stone,
the vision
that pounds your skull.

The sky will not yield:
the day drums down.

Last Look at La Plata, Missouri

The park, the heart, you see at town's center is soft
underfoot. All winter long the dying bluegrass
has fed on cicada bones, enough to fill a loft:

the drone of dying, constant cymbals and hard bass,
recedes to a waning echo in your ear. Each year
the town drops an inch or two in the mud, and has

little sense of its going, though a certain fear
of losing trade caused the Palace to buy a shade
and paint the yellow Open sign and sell kids beer.

The town speaks of history, and goes slightly mad.
The silver jet, the town's only hero's joke it's said,
has lost a tire; the fuselage and wing tanks, glad

for past skies, are captive to flung rocks and love-red
names. Summer was too long and heavy for the white
bandstand warping above lost chords and maidenheads.

The town affirms its past. The druggist kills his light
above the store. A diesel moans toward Kansas City.
A lone dog barks. A child cries. All of a winter night.

Return to La Plata, Missouri

The warping bandstand reminds you of the hard rage
you felt in the heart of the town the day you said goodbye
to the park, silver jet, and cicadas dead in the sage.

The town is basic red, although it browns. A cry
of murder, rape, or wrong will always bend the night
hard into the broken grass. You listen close for sighs

of lovers on the ground. The darkness gathers light
and throws it down: something glows that you cannot name,
something fierce, abstract, given time and space you might

on a journey leave behind, a stone to carve your fame
on, or a simple word like *love*. The sun is down
or always going down in La Plata, the same

sun. Same too the child's cry that turns the mother's frown
brittle as chalk or the town's face against the moon.
Same too the moan of dog and diesel circling the town

in an air so heavy with cloud that there is little room
for breath or moon. Strange: in a town so country, so
foreign, you never hear a song nor see a loom

pattern dark threads into a history you would know
and would not know. You think you see one silver star.
But the town offers only itself, and you must go.

An Ex–Deputy Sheriff Remembers the Eastern Oklahoma Murderers

1. Summerfield

They took a tire tool to his head,
this gentle stranger from Wyoming.
Oh, we caught them over
at Talihina drinking beer
at Lester's Place, calling
the myna bird bad names
and shooting shuffleboard.
I'm telling you
they were meek in the muzzle
of our guns. They claimed innocence
and: why, they went fishing
with the Cowboy just the other day.
We said we knew, knew too
the way they stole him blind
that night. We spoke of blood,
the way the dogs had lapped his face.
The youngest of the three bad brothers,
barely thirteen, began to cry:
"He told us everything was all right
and we hit him till he died."
And that is how it was,
a simple thing, like breathing,
they hit him until he died,
until he bled Wyoming dry
there on the road
in that part of Oklahoma
no stranger has ever owned.

2. Red Oak

We shot the Choctaw way back in '94,
last legal execution by firing squad.
He didn't die, through the heart, square
and he didn't die.
The high sheriff, my old boss,
stuffed his own shirt down
the Choctaw's neck
to stop the rattle in his throat.
You couldn't shoot a downed man
no matter what and he had to die.
Damned good Choctaw, I'll say that.
Red Oak had no jail and it was too
blasted cruel to execute him
before his crop was in. The judge
scheduled it for the fall, first Saturday
after the corn was in the Choctaw's crib.
That damned fool Choctaw gathered
his corn like any other dirt farmer,
dressed clean, and kept his word.
"I'm ready" is all he said that day.
You got to admire a man like that,
Indian or not, murderer or just plain fool.
He'd shot three men for sleeping
in his barn and taking the milk bucket
away from his little girl, though she
wasn't harmed at all, and he showed up
just like he'd said he would.

                        There
was a picnic in the shade after we choked
the Choctaw to death and took the rifle home.
First time I'd ever seen a camera,
big damned black thing on legs,
smelled like seven kinds of sin every time
it popped. Had fresh hominy and chicken and the last
of some damned fine late sweet red watermelons.

3. LeFlore

Goddamnest thing I ever saw
was when old Mac ran down that poor old LeFlore boy.
Old Mac was drunk as thunder
when we chained him to the tree
he'd just pissed on back of his house.
Said he'd wanted to see what it was like
to bounce a man off the hood
of the truck he hauled pulpwood on.
No other reason than just that.
Hell of a note, but I've heard worse.
They all have got some sort of song and dance.
Old Mac's kids were screaming louder
than the crows and threatening us with garden hoes.
We shooed them off with fake fast draws.
That poor old LeFlore boy was as deaf as stone,
a condition they say came with the color of his skin,
though as mild in his ways as the first fall winds.
Old Mac had hit him from behind. Coming
down the gravel road, lord, he must have been
doing sixty and with a full two-cord load.
Hit him dead on. Center. Cracked his
back in half all the way through. That poor
old LeFlore boy's rubber boots were
left standing exactly where he last had stood.
How can you account for that, those silly
rubber boots standing bolt upright
dead in the middle of the goddamned road?

4. Wister

What made him think he could get away with it
is beyond me. Hell, he'd lived over at Glendale
all his life. Everybody knew he had a stiff
little finger on his right hand. The mask hid
nothing, not even the fear and tobacco juice
he always drooled out the corners of his mouth.
He shot the teller right between the eyes and

made the others strip. Don't ask why. Cleaned
out the vault of a thousand dollars, mostly
fives, and made it fifty yards down the Frisco
tracks before Mathes, the bank's owner, naked
as a jaybird and pissing a blue streak, blew
his left shoulder off with a 30.06. I've got
the cartridge shell to this day. Was going to
have one of them little lighters, size of your
finger, made out of it. But I decided to quit.

Autobiography, Chapter 7: Home for Memorial Day

The names that trust their bones to this hot hill
> have learned the rage of stone and pine. The wind
> that brings the morning into your eyes says live.
> You try a stone, find it rooted past your years.
> You question why you came. The answer comes out
> wrong as the women you haven't seen since hot sin
> was in your groin. Belovéd, Gone From This World,
> in weeds. Gold in a mourner's teeth names you fool.

Years past they used to spread a picnic under pines,
> sing hymns that sparked a bright beyond, and lovers
> rolled on stones and needles fierce to skin. You feel
> yourself in somebody else's dream: one friend whose
> hello is too far away to see, relatives too golden to
> touch, the *Requiescat in Pace* no foreigner can read.

You tell the fat friend you no longer know your life
> and see your epitaph in his handful of white roses.
> The way he hides his flowers behind somebody's name
> makes you feel the shame. His Belovéd cannot be read
> because of weeds. You want to touch his stone, tell
> him: we have endured. But you say something vague —
> yesterday's weather, God — customary words to exit on.

TWO

Death by Water

In the after-death state the deceased imagines that he has a physical body, though he has been severed therefrom by the high surgery of death.
—Sir John Woodroffe, introduction to the *Tibetan Book of the Dead*

Sundown at Swan Lake, Missouri

At the lake's edge
I face the west
and count
last waves
dying in the sun.

The speedboats' rip
recedes
to the far edge
of my inner ear.
The wake vanishes.

Stones turn cold
beneath my feet.
The day falls
as fast as
a hawk to prey.

I do not want
to be anywhere
except here:
the waves
cease to break

and last birds
glide unruffled
at my feet
across the constant
plain of sky.

My eyes are full
of the silver
of water, a smooth
metal drawing
my hands

to the test
I refuse
to take:
I will not drown
to know my life.

The Body Falters

The forest thickens
my blood. I stumble
on acorns grown
the size of apples,
sticks no larger
than the gnat's eye.
I am animal
in this old darkness
I have not known
for years. The body
falters, the mind
joins the earth.
The sound of crawling
cracks my ears
and of the lively trees,
the brown, brown grass,
and the one voice
of the steady river.
I have never been
anywhere but here,
flat on my stomach
embracing the constant
earth, this world
I hold. Sky on my back
I feel the needled wheel
of stars tracking
my skin with pores
deep as moonlight.
My eyes break into
the earth, into
the dark alluvial
blood. Beyond
this place:

only another
and another
and another.
I am repeated
into the earth.

On the Eve of My Parents' Sixtieth Anniversary

I wake to the way:
the road stretches out
like a knotted thread,

the towns' eyes
I have to
live through.

Woven into
these hard lives
I know myself
by the pattern
of roads,

the tapestried earth,
the maze of ends.

I come bearing
the only gift
I have:

this handful
of loneliness,
sheared
like loose ends
from the clothes
of strangers.

Old Soldiers' Home at Marshalltown, Iowa

No movement on the hill: the old soldiers
are dying, dying into mushrooms they dream.
On the grounds near the rising river, the slow
phallic plants grow white and low. The days
swell, and no one stoops to the task at hand.

The old soldiers are dying, dying into the spring:
statues turn green with the grass. The tavern
at 13th and Summit echoes this green death,
but there is no song of esprit de corps,
no body lying on the floor drunk on
a reverie of a Flanders field or Argonne.

Even the drugstore across from the gate
is as vacant as the eyes you sometimes see
at the dark windows on the hill. The years
have emptied Seberg's of more than wares.
Time was when Jean Seberg was a bedside name,
the darling of bored veterans and gossips in
this town, the star of Saturday matinees.

From the tavern stool, you listen to the whir
of the laundromat across the street washing
some lonely nurse's whites, spinning them free
of trenches, the soiled touch she's come to dread.
You know that you've got it wrong, dead wrong,
that life here is as vital as your organs.
But somewhere in your head the old soldiers
are dying, dying into the fullness of spring.

Swan Lake, Again

I name this lake
a wash for tired eyes,

a balm for the poor
Galahad, the quester

I am for words.
There's something in

the blood that draws
the water to my eyes,

something that knows
the slightest of things

must be named.
Even the snake

down there, down there,
curling through my hair.

There are dreams
of water

snakes have
I can never know,

but when you
curl through me,

I feel my marrow twist,
old friend,

brother to my blood,
sworn enemy of heels.

Pyramid Lake, Late Summer

The stone shore
cracks with
the sinking years:

fissures fan out
and map the heavy sky,
the broken water,

even
write your name
in arabesques

you are afraid
to trace. An ancient fear
grooves your face.

At your back
somewhere, near,
the desert grows.

Beyond your eyes
the water strikes
the sky into waves.

You will leave
this place now,
but first

you will,
stone by stone, take
away your name.

For a Drowned Sailor, Age 4

Times
the drowned child
fades into your dream
of fish, you let
the line go slack
and try not to snag
the smallest limb.
Your arms sink.
Now, the news
he cannot be found
stays the rod. Death
by water, the loveliest
of deaths by far,
rainbows
you cannot dream.
Now into sundown
the mother sounds
for the lost child.
Though you no longer
see the boat, her face,
blank as the last dull
light, will not fade.
You no longer hear
her cry, hear only
a lowing
across the water,
like soft cannon,
a lowing
carrying miles
across the water.

Elegy for the Girl Who Drowned at Goats Bluff

The sun strikes water like soft stone,
oblique and torn by surface waves.
Below, in the still place of stone,
the slow fish nuzzle through the caves

you seldom know are there at all
and rest among the drowned girl's bones.
Above, the bluff is too brittle
for a date in stone. The long day downs,

and she alone records the passing.
You think you know her now, the scream
that cracked the bluff, the siren song
that wails its way into the dream

you sometimes have. Dark water.
Darker still the night. You wait
for the water to take the sky, for
the floating moon to turn stone white

as the skin of dead fish. You know
she sees you stranger to this place,
her empty eyes wide against the night,
her empty hands, her empty face.

Postcard to Grace Schulman

Here in this fireplace the flame dies into
ash and the night closes in, gray, winged:
a silent, deadly air as heavy as old snow.
I must write you, now, that your felt presence
is enough, that the stilling voice of your poems
goes the way of fire, consumes, and is done,
that the voice sings through wood, andiron, attic
flue, and what's left is the heavy weight of ash,
an old snow for old men to worship in.
Clothed in this mourning air, I kneel here to
find one coal, one burning wing of light,
an affirmation. Something as inexplicable
as words has risen through my open hands.

Autobiography, Chapter 17: Floating the Big Piney

How the river cools your blood is something you can't
    explain: you search the bottom stones for words
    unscientific, words fleshed with the sound of sense,
    maybe a chant laid upon the water the time
    words were all and fathers sang their sons ways
    to be and the river flowed sure of its pace.

You lie back in the canoe. Your own child points the bow
    now into the blue breath of sky: trees course
    overhead, and your eyes bend with pillars
    of air, the cornering birds; you lie back into
    the dream you know you'll have just once, a token
    from a far time, a river you can't explain.

All words are lost and you want to sing the meaning
    and origin of things, to make an appositive
    of light, something solid as a stone to hand
    this man-child. But all you have to offer is
    pause, the silence of water and the small
    knowledge that the river takes you over all.

Scouting Tom Fry Hollow

The trail in I blazed on pine is gone
without a trace. The lay of the land and sky
has run amuck. I check the ridge south,
look for marks I know cannot be there now.

One thing remains unchanged. The hollow hard
below: the brown, brown grass flowing around
chimney rubble and collapsed corral, the sound
of distant wolves keening in the stony hills.

I go down, as before, to look for the grave
I will not find again. The wind always
blows and sundown comes hours ahead of time.
Little chance any artifact is left

to clear the name of bones the hollow bears.
Grave unmarked, the hanged man still hangs under
the ghost of every tree. I raise a stone,
poor homage, for the next man to wonder on.

On Top of Winding Stair Mountain

Halfway done with this mountain,
I stuff wild berries into my mouth
like a starving coon chased to bone.
As far as I can see is blue.
I swallow the space of valleys
and grow drunk with the vision
that blues my eyes. I feel
my lips, my tongue, my throat
assuming the color of air.
Shadows nest in my ears.

High on this mountain, my hands
are scarred from feathers or fear
I would give lives to remember.
I reach for the sun, crazy with
the moment, and somewhere there
is an echo of a crash, a sound
of broken water, a far cry
through silence. My legs are stone
as bedrock. I turn back, hand
and mouth, to berries as a lone
hawk plummets into the world.

Under Buffalo Mountain

The prairie flows toward
the sacred lake

where the silent water
waits, deep

in its secret of geese,
for the coming of snow.

Here the Choctaw stopped, forever,
staked the ground

with bones broken beyond rage.
Blood hides

in these hills and haunts
the faded town:

the drunk drowns in sleep,
the geese forget to come,

the snow falls,
and the moon is down.

Autobiography, Chapter 14: Tombstone at Petit Bay, near Tahlequah*

Looking for artifacts that map your world less real,
    you find the obelisk, dwarfed among the weeds;
    knee-high and almost growing from the chert
    hillside, it hides its legend like night the
    features of a face.

You read the date, 1839. And the one faint vertical
    word, *child*, in Sikwayi script. The grave where
    no grave should be gently shocks your senses
    clean: each fracture of chert is bone. You feel
    a sudden reverence for all stone.

Years you've quested in these hills, a running search
    for something still you cannot name—something
    holy, proof of migration or lost Phoenician sailors.

You are tempted toward a gentle excavation, but know
    you will not dig into the earth for the same
    reason you never move the soil except to plant.

The obelisk casts a shadow longer than its length.
    The narrow darkness leans along the hill, toward
    the bay and the slow moon rising from the fabled
    east.

---

*Tahlequah, capital of the Cherokee Nation; also reputed to mean "one got lost."

Still-Hildreth Sanitarium: Ice Fishing

Huddled like a lost child round his knees,
I cover the hole I hacked in the ice.
Like an idiot I would know the secret
of fish. Here in the middle of the solid
lake, the fish I take are pale with
the cold fever of winter, their scales
shocked at 5 below into fast freeze.

The sanitarium at my back is dead
against the frozen sky. I try
to visualize a sun, one to burn
my head clear of ice, clear of broken
glass and the footless shoe I saw
last fall where the lilies now lie dead.
Cold this lake has always been: cold then
with swimmers numbed by electric shock,
cold now from arctic ice, from window
panes sucked down by a force I cannot
read, from ghosts wandering on the hill.

To come here in dead of winter
is to die or know the quality of ice.
You have to watch your mind. I still
can see the agony and the pain
plain on many a face that ever
did time here. But tell yourself: given
another life, you could have lost
your sins here. The sky is blank,
will stay blank until the season shocks
itself sensible again, until the fish
no longer freeze in the hook of my hand.

Autobiography, Chapter 6: San Diego Harbor at Dusk

On the horizon, stars break through the fog; below the hotel,
> the *Star of India* lists against the pier under a growing
> heaviness of spent lives.

The steel hull strains under the thunder of the distant seas,
> the harsh light of the shore, the broken wind fit for
> no sail.

The masts and beams turn salt with the barnacle years: the ship
> waits for the fullness of dark and one last voyage down
> the other side of the sky, one last captain, one last crew,
> and the last of pilgrims wanting only the openness of sea.

The harbor grows with the dusk, and ghosts ride the tide and town,
> immigrant souls wandering the foreign edge waiting for the
> passage that will not come.

For these souls this poem, poor payment for what I cannot give:
> a promise of sails. For this is no hell and I no master
> of ships.

Tracking the Siuslaw Man

FOR LETHE EASTERLING

Ice honed by wind
is sharp with messages from the north.
Firs split under silver blades,
and tracks are fossils under glass.

You read the rigid trail
under a sun dead as amber,
tell yourself the cold you feel
can't touch the fear

in the marrow of your bones.
Siuslaw passed this way is what you know
from footprints hairy with frost
and shadows in the wood that will not freeze.

The trail always ends
on solid stone mute with glyphs
that send you back centuries
or into a dream you never want to have.

You hack the last print
from the glazed ground, feel it shatter
in your hand while somewhere
a dark Siuslaw raven calls

and snow men bend to the task of mountains.

San Miguel de Allende

In San Miguel de Allende
you count the stars by twos.

Even the moon's a lover,
Mars at her lips.

A sagging Mary hangs on the wall
with her stone Jesus.

Nobody's ever alone
in this place of echoes.

Once in a rare sundown
we saw the clouds twice catch fire,

one sun trailing the other down
like a red pariah dog.

The Last Trip Somewhere West

On the freeway,
heading west,

I run through
miles of sun,

the road behind
passing away

like the light,
until the sun

beats me down,
stands dead still

west of me,
then drops below

the day's last edge.
I bury

my eyes
in the night

and drive toward
the road's end.

Autobiography, Chapter 16: Return to Rich Mountain

This is the spot where you killed yourself with bad gin,
    the phony suicide you thought would work.
    That's past, and you'd like to say you've grown
    new feet to grip this everlasting earth.
    No, you're no lizard that in losing a leg
    grows another newer, better than before.

Ghosts and prophecies flood your mind, but you're no saint.
    You proved it then, and now you'll never brag
    you held the day or ever stopped the sun
    while walls crumbled and the old queen's summer castle,
    now restored, sank into the dust. A long
    day of abdication in '48.
    Wilhelmina's long gone. God save the Queen.
    Her last stone castle runes this mountainside.

The only thing you've grown is a salty set of eyes.
    You see this pirated mountain earth alive
    with forebears, Indians gathering herbs for cure.
    You're blind to Sunday traffic from Little Rock,
    and the work you have to do to live and love,
    still another philosophy in stone.
    You come here to contemplate your only fame,
    a wandering Dutchman, world without an end.

This day is as wide and open as it ever was.
    The dark ascends, a vast sea of water,
    even before the sun goes down. You leave
    the hot cot and ask your legs to verify
    the sinking earth. Somewhere far off below
    in the real land the sad twang of mandolins
    tells you this is no foreign country now.
    The pines are here, the needles in your hair.

Comcomly's Skull

Comcomly's skull is coming home.
That wily one-eyed Chinook chief,
whose other bones are scattered from
the grave, keeper of slaves, thief,
will have his fore-flattened skull
and, gods willing, his fevered soul

back, buried finally and forever,
courtesy Ilwaco, Wash., Cemetery
Association. According to Meriweather,
head of the Chinook Council, "We
plan, for the event, a salmon bake;
we'll call it Chief Comcomly Day."

August 12. Slow birds tread the sun
above the open grave. The priest—
Baptist or Episcopalian,
pagan or seventh son of Crow—casts
a shadow too long for the time
of day. His eulogy turns on rhyme.

After salmon and wine, song birds
and a soft coastal rain begin.
The sun has sunk into the clouds.
Somewhere over against a mountain
a lone wolf lets out one wild howl.
The earnest sky begins to fall.

An unexpected hail. Hell
on dogs and birds. The sky can't hold
its wrath or praise long enough for all
this pomp and circumstance to mold
ancestral flesh onto his skull.
The eyes stay empty. The sky grows full.

Autobiography, Chapter 15: Agate Beach, California

Hanging on the edge of the world, I bat my eyes;
    the world stays firm, though this wild sea
    is a vision I'll never comprehend. Gull cries
    and breakers beating at my brain take the black
    beach like a storm of vampire wings. The great
    gray mound of water is total grave.

I came to see the sea, and now what I see is a crystal
    fear growing in my groin. This ocean is a lead
    lid on the coffin of the world, the sun a burning
    stake through the heart. I am diminished by the
    view. Dead eyes crowd the beach, agates clouded
    by the pale geography of time. Crab shells, sand
    dollars, a broken conch, and there near the last
    hard ebb: *my* bones.

Bones trembling still under the spell of the sea, I
    calm them, little white deaths that have known
    this west, in my entirely human hands. I throw
    them out to sea, finding that after all I still
    am grounded in sacrifice.

A suicide no doubt in less than twenty years, I'll
    not go easy, hoping all along something like
    this ill-named pacific shroud will toss me up
    again, as undead as each ninth wave and as
    inexplicable.

The Only Photograph of Quentin at Harvard

FOR DAN RECTOR

On the far left, at the edge,
a pair of hands holds
an open book.

At the right-hand bottom corner
a pair of shoes hangs
pegged to the wall,

the soles outward and soiled.
At the end of a word Shreve laces
his hands in his lap.

Central, across the checkered table,
Quentin counts the silence in his throat
below a half-

curtained bookcase. A mirror
reflects pictures pyramided
up a wall.

The one window is draped in white
gauze. Time is stilled
forever

in a hushed tone of sand.
The hands are about
to turn a page.

THREE
Ishmael

Myth is that which is taken for granted when thought begins.
—*Encyclopaedia Britannica*

My Father's House

1.

Below my father's house
are many meadows,

and beyond the meadows
the pawpaw trees

line the river banks.

I am alone here
where my father's voice

drifts, a small cloud,
in a sky too bright,

in a river far too clear.

2.

What echoes there are
are here below

my father's house
among the pawpaw trees,

the shadowing leaves.

I am alone here,
stranger to words

and worlds I'll never know;
like the fruit of these trees

I grow soft

3.

in summer wind,
remembering the firm

time, the sound of bells
in the meadows,

the lowing herds.

The dream ongoing,
the found past,

the one shadow
I always walk in,

my father's house.

Origin

Find a word
you haven't said or signed.

Farm it through
the very terraces of lung,
the steppes of eyes;
and watch a certain power grow,
an origin, a stem.

For there is a chemistry
to words:

how, for instance,
the saliva rises
to the tongue
as the word forms
like a cake
midthroat;

how, too,
the teeth grow
sharp
as the word
falls from the lips
like a green apple.

Molecular
as helix or hell,
words hold together even

stuff the deaf-mute's made of:
a tree of fingers,
a lace of flesh.

The Good Dark

East of the house
the frogs on the pond
prime the clouds
with thunder
under windy cattails.

The whole sky
boils black
as gunpowder
in the summer roll
of drums.

The rabbits
out of your garden
dive into little houses
under the grass,

and, surely, like you
gather the good dark
of home
about them
and sing
in the bombardment
of rain.

Tonight the Moon

FOR CAROLYN

Tonight the moon comes red,
climbs on the earth's turning,
fades toward the white reflection
of your eyes.

        Love, this night
is a night for holding the moon
like a fragile glass of wine.

I will take your white arms
as the moon claims our skin.

Inside my bones the marrow
maps the vintage sky.

I feel, Love, I feel
our passing as the moon passes,

and I will hold you, Love,
all the moons our bodies
complete themselves into,
into the final cast of moon.

Autobiography, Chapter 13: Ghost Train, the Dream

For years that train drove every night, and its low
    dirge of steam filled the wind with a song
    beginning way beyond my eyes.

Always far off north of home, where the bottomlands
    were heavy with two slow rivers, where the cane-
    brakes splayed away into the weeping woman's slough,
    the distant roar of fire and steel drummed me nightly
    into dream.

I was cadenced by that dark engine off the edge of
    night into the dream of a drowned son, and am
    cadenced still.

For when the wind rises nights I cannot sleep, there's
    a certain droning in the air that wakes my bones:

I see the black hulk looming through the dark, its
    drivers pounding black smoke white against the
    weeping woman's moon,

and still I am lifted from myself and wailed away over
    dark water like some other mother's son.

After Dreams

FOR CAROLYN

In dreams
I have flown
into myself,
through lands
heavy with
the lead
of nights
of no moon.

Soon now
I shall settle
softly down
like the down
of goslings
in no wind.

I shall pillow
my head with
your soft form
and wake in
the high blue
air of morning.

The Ghost's Story I

What I wanted to do was only this:
touch the tender nape of your neck.

You moved away, never knowing me.
My hand is suspended in the light air,

still, of your passing. Your aura
holds my fingers in light repose,

the soft, gray air of morning framing
the bones, the flesh, in a pale wash

of blue, like the photo of a hand
that was never really there at all.

After a Postcard from Stryk in Japan

Lucien, all
the green river,
falling
green beneath
the green bridge,

all
the green houses,
their windows
opening light
onto the river

falling
now beyond
the green bridge
into the green sky,

and now
          all
                  quiet
the green night blossoms.

Autobiography, Chapter 12: Hearing Montana

FOR BOB CONLEY

The distance drums your words into my ears; it's good
    to hear your voice backed by the force of snow.

I speak of things small enough to ride the wires and
    the Dakota winds. I try to find a certain power of
    words to make the distance thin.

And growing in my ears are the sounds I think we know:
    the flight of low geese, the awesome scream of
    owls, the sudden fall of skree.

I name these things with my weaker words, but feel a
    need to chant until the magic of my voice
    strikes me dumb as stone.

Words are sacred, friend, you remind me once again.
    I hear the cadence dancing on the wires and
    some other voices dimly cutting in

humming the weather, ways to know the snow, something
    with love in it, god knows what, as if these
    other voices are also somehow dimly you.

In Rudolph's Cave

In the cave
Rudolph found,
the walls hug
you like skin.
You fall
like a bucket
down vertical
stone and el east
into a devil's wedge
toward dark morning.
When finally
you crawfish
back, stand
and look
into the well
you must climb,
the amazement
in your mouth
is blinding.
There at
the bottom
of the shaft
into sky,
there, there,
on the still
blue surface
is one
pinpoint
of white.

Autobiography, Chapter 3: Nearing El Paso

Into the brown sundown, we are free-falling, the bus
 sinking toward an illimitable offing of dusk,
 down, down with the sun.

Setting out is like this: you must acknowledge the horizon
 and count the hills you have to count.

Dream is part of it: you become that which you see, grow
 wise as stones, talk crow with birds.

And it all makes sense, even the salt wind off the blank
 face of Guadeloupe.

Everything is new, strange: you know it, it knows you.

Dog Days 1978

An affliction so general you find no name
to cover the pain: dog days in Missouri, same
low dull sky, the repetitive gray that clouds
every window, every pond, the very clods

in fields that die into a memory of autumn.
Dog days linger. The fire of frost to come
hardly attracts you at all, at all, so strong
is desire coursing your blood, in this long

time. Daily you look for words, but what you
always see is the cryptic flight of blue-
black birds against the gray, the invisible
script you are never fast enough or able

to read. And so. And so the days hang above
you, meaningless as the adolescent love
among the weathering stalks of corn. You mourn
these days, and every day you end with pain,

with desire swollen within that will pass
only with the season, the first death of grass,
of the stalks of corn, among which the farm girl names
her quick pain and the boy knows the power in his name.

One for Grand Ronde, Oregon

> I gave them fire . . . , blind hope.
> —Aeschylus, *Prometheus Bound*

Ghosts of dead loggers haunt the night
where General Sheridan drove the light
into the last warring tribes. Grand Ronde
lies lead under the hoot-owl moon.

Indians and loggers die here still.
Years ago Big Moose drank his fill
of rotgut, told it like it was,
told them all to go to hell because

they were. The mountain called him up,
shook his senses clean, and let him jump.
Others still can hear his dark call
the nights the sky begins to fall.

No one has the guts to say where's hope.
Crow's a poor savior anymore. Croak
and feathers made the night. But now
what's left? The flayed god and the scowl

on the face of Spirit Mountain. The moon
is never right: the blood's too soon
for sacrifice and the constant rain
pounds like a wedge into the brain.

There's not one soul left in this town
who does not try to pray the frown
off the stone face the mountain's made
of: give us this day, god knows we've paid.

Autobiography, Chapter 18: Camp in the Dead of Summer

The low sky settles lower on the trees, a dusk as humid
   and salt as equatorial wind. There is no wind to
   trade for rain. The limbs lash your face. You count
   yourself, among the sweating blessed, a pilgrim
   through the heavy green: gnarled oaks and witch
   hazel, those silent screams, armed with arrows
   pointing ways. The lost parent guided to his own
   true son, bivouacked in a wilderness you would
   not have him lose or leave for love nor honey of
   a civilizing kiss. It's hell these summer days,
   this treading air to stay alive as far as any camp.

You could die here without tears or sweat enough to keep
   you cool. Lack of wind is wrong. Something is lying
   ill at ease on land. The last night's retreat, and
   you face the flags, absent among the scouts in stiff
   salute. It's hard to face the fire and your son's
   cloudless eyes. What you have lost is also his to lose.
   You dread obituaries, wonder how you ever lived as
   innocent and wild as the weathering stone his fire
   is backed by. You long for home, that sanctuary of
   loss. You listen with your humming ears to his rare
   enthusiastic woe: his tale of trials among the caves

and other rituals he was honored in. All his badges are
   stitched in green thread: an innocence of rage and
   insects. You cannot tell him once you touched a
   nesting hawk, slept alone seven nights under a canopy
   of cracking trees, falling stars, that wild-woman
   moon gone mad. A vision hard to call back now that
   the earth turns and the world is real with dollars
   and horse sense. You misremember most bad dreams:
   to stay alive you have to sing and lie. His words

pass into your eyes. Or maybe it's sweat that stings.
The words move in, and night moves west with your
life. You anticipate a descending wind. You shake
his hand scoutwise. It's dry and flesh, the squeeze
a kiss of bones. You say goodbye the best you can,
tell him to obey the lay of land and time. You
mean it the way you think you lived and daily died.

Lost in Sulphur Canyons

All the stones
unturned say
you are alone.

Not even a sun
cracks
the lead sky.

The deer
you thought
you tracked
has never known
the stones
you step on.

Stone by stone
you follow
the small water
down through
sulphur springs
rank as the fear
you try not
to taste.

For such descent
as this, you need
a guide, someone
to lean a word
or curse on.

Only the stones
know your breath
is wrong.

An absence
of wind grays
the pines
and your hair.

You stoop
to drink
your face.

The sweet, white
bite of water
leaves you stunned.

You smile to see
a face pale
against the sky,
a smile
you never knew
was there at all.

With all the hell
of sulphur and pitch
you know somehow
you couldn't be
happier, lost
as a stray dog
among the stones.

Autobiography, Chapter 9: Leaving, Again

You've got to leave this land again before it hurts
    you into a sin the years will not ease: a constant
    fear swells in your groin, and there's a singing
    in the trees your blood wants to beat time to.

Easy it would be to stay and dream, to walk-wolf these
    woods and fields, to play what you've always been
    and are afraid to be. You know there's a crescendo
    building in your blood, a raging conquistador, wild
    sailor, part pilgrim looking for a mecca he'll never
    find. Or find and lose and find again.

Dreams you once had in a bad time come back to haunt
    your ears: sounds of music too sensual for light
    drum dark in the soft trees, and the leaves begin
    again to dance and shapes take form, lovely and
    green.

You see the muddy river clear, sirens naked on its banks.
    A wild urge silent on their lips tells you plain this
    land will always sing you back, quick with dream, your
    hands always poised for overture.

The Iowa Sequence

1. Waterloo

Stranger to
the moated center,
I try to mold
my face native.
Full of trees,
my eyes are quick
to show the lie.
The poet I came
to hear beats time
to traffic as foreign
as my mind.
I find no common ground.
The artificial lake,
its wind and waves,
are distance
I cannot bridge.
His words do not
walk water.

2. Marshalltown

Christ would like
hanging here:
the sky portends
earthquake.
There's a heavy air
at noon, thick as oil,
entombed thunder from
mountains glaciered
flat and black.

Jean Seberg's hometown
and bête noire, a town
to leave your sins in,
from where every road
goes up.

3. Muscatine

Home of mustard and melons,
cradle of rats and river,
your façades speak
of better times, windows
cracked, blued brittle
by this awful wind.
Your one fat street,
a tongue black with names
old as vinegar,
crosses your one steepled hill
and falls straight
into the Mississippi.

4. Mason City

The museum here
preserves the heart
of Iowa: an unfinished
eighteenth-century portrait
details a face in
white, the features
as serene as death mask.
Nothing is complete
except the face, the face:
all else a shroud of lines.

5. Nora Springs

They say Indians
washed away their sins
here; that's why
the river stinks.
The fish I catch
are cancerous and black.
I haven't seen
the sun in weeks.
The river does not run.
There's a general
sinking of the ground.
I think I hear
the natives praying.

Autobiography, Chapter 11: Prelude to Writing

I am dreaming. I am sitting here dreaming. It is raining
and a good time for dreaming. I do not know whether
the poetry will come today. If it does, I will be
ready for it.

I think it is going to come soon. There was an image of a
footbridge a moment's eye ago, and a river under it.
The water was still with a scum on it, and what looked
like, from that distance, a paper boat. It could have
been a paper sack. But that doesn't matter. Sack or boat.

A limestone bluff to the north. I think I see a cave, wild
flowers at the mouth. Steps leading down from the top.
I walk down them. Someone has lived in this place. In
powdered stone, the soft imprint of a thigh. Ants trail
across the dunes.

Strange how the wind writes on water. The wind carries the
scum away, and the sky floats by the mouth of the cave.
Someone is looking out across the river. It must be me,
but I do not know the eyes. They are a long way back,
and they see only the reflection on the water, not the
water itself. They are looking at the falling sky.

The water is suddenly white with geese, which see something
startling. The geese do not fly; they paddle dumb and
careful circles around one another, timing each stroke
with the certainty of flight. I am sure of one thing:
they want to know what it is amazes them before they
try the heavy sky.

On the bridge, someone has left a grandfather's clock. Its
face is peeling in the rain, and the short hand is
missing. I turn the key: there is an odd sound, like
sunlight striking leaves, or kisses in dark old doorways.
Something is going to start in a minute if I keep turning
the key.

10–4–76
Mason City, Iowa

Memoirs of a Catskinner

We downed the cathedral
with ball and crane.
I confessed just once
to a flying saint,
then swore silence
in the nauseous dust.

All day I dreamed
quiet prairies, wild
chicory and coneflowers.

Splinters
from stained glass
and falling gargoyles
shrouded my green glasses,
and Lord
the noise: the yellow cat
knocking pews
seven ways to Sunday.

I consecrated meadows
in my head,
counted gopher holes.

The foreman jumped my ass
at lunch for backtracking
onto the street: Keep it
on holy ground, he said.
I genuflected.
He twirled the masonic ring,
third finger, right hand.

Toward sundown
I took the altar
into my blade
and fishes fell.

O Lord, I yelled
in the bursting air,
let my eardrums fail
forever
in some other world.

I herded sheep
through red clover
and silent wind,
columns of steady air.

I dozed into the vacant crypt,
and prayed:
Let them dig my grave
by hand
O Lord.

On the Bridge at Fourche Maline River

Forty feet below, the water stands as dull
as dog days. No movement toward the lake
ten snaking miles away. You stand here full
of hope you have always been told to have,
with no regard for the ruined years, those rabid
foxes at your heels.

     You stop here whenever
you have the time. The river's pull is strong.
The dark water, too thick and slow to reflect
anything outside itself, sends a constant song.
Worlds away you always know the river
is your home. You've never seen the river
run toward its sea. Yet it moves at the touch
when you take time to go down, lay your hands
on the warm river, and speak to the current
that flows into and through your blood.

          It has
been years since you swam this muddy stream
and, bearing a rock for ballast, walked the bottom
straight across, bank to bank, in the longest breath
you ever held. Time and time again, as now,
you dream that walk. This time it's real. You leave
your clothes flapping on the rail and jump, wide,
into the warm water and feel the river
bottom wrap a gentle skin about your feet.
As you break upward for breath, you taste
the sweet meat of earth the river is made of,
and you remember the earth and that you are home.

The Last Chance

The myna bird speaks
of love. His whistle
cuts into the bone
ears of a whitetail's
head stuffed above
the bar.

Fifty miles the county's
dry. You stop here
to tell yourself
go home, but hear
the black experience
of a goddamned bird

whose hello sucks
at the marrow
of your bones.
You wonder how a soul
can pass from
his beak and break

upon your face, split
the whiskers you grew
to be wise in. You wonder
at his avalanche of words,
the last drink you took,
the dance on your skin

you can't beat time to.
You wonder, but you
do not ask. You
listen hard with
your cracking eyes.
He asks about your life.

You tell him lies
while he prunes
a feather, lets it drop.
Your life is sour
in the glass. Crow
made the earth and all

things therein, brought fire.
This bird's a ghost
you tell your sins.
Nobody is listening.
Outside, the sun falls
into the brittle grass.

FOUR

Night Falls, Ritual and Fast

After everything ends
and even while the story goes on
I accept all that is left over.
   —William Stafford, "The Whole Story"

Year's End 1977

> One must have a mind of winter.
> —Wallace Stevens

The moon lies to the bedded snow:
the all-night dawn is as good as day.
This is the mind of winter that you have come to know.

All night long you have looked for the right
words to rid your mind of all the day
in order to see the nothing that is of a winter's night.

The silence upon the fields holds you
in its steady light, and your eyes
become the nothing of light you try to see clearly through.

The vision blurs in blowing snow:
zodiacs of flake and wind take
orbit in your mind, and something final begins to grow,

the long year's end. You cannot stay
blank as winterscape and survive
the lesson of snow, the igloo of ice that domes the winter's day.

All that is told in the nothing that is
escapes you in the breath you take,
but breathe you will this winter's night the nothing that surely is.

Winter Pastoral *

The tracks in snow cut the hill in half,
and the hunter draws his bow. A bath
of light, shuddered from the frozen moon,
washes his shoulders white, gathers
the shadows tightly as a loom.

His hands are constantly in place.
A rapid sound of broken ice
cracks the timber on the hill,
then recedes with the cautious pace
of animals weaving past a kill.

And now the hunter's moon is down.
The snow is dark where the tracks wound
the fading light. The silence of snow,
the soft thread, once again is spun
by the breath of stars the hunter knows.

Contemporary Native American Poetry

For one thing, you can believe it:
the skin chewed soft enough to wear,
the bones hewn hard as a totem
from hemlock. It's a kind of scare-

crow that will follow you home nights.
You've seen it ragged against a field,
but you seldom think, at the time,
to get there it had to walk through hell.

Midwest Midwinter

1.

You know it's true the sky has fallen:
a blue has settled upon the ground
and gray fields grow solid overhead.
Points of light, thousands, break behind your eyes.
A nova whirls about your nose.
Your mind implodes, black hole in space,
and draws all sound and sense
to a center you never want to be.

2.

The hard gravity of ice holds you down.
Days like this it's hard to move.
Landscape is constantly the same.
You envy Venezuelans the warmer world.
You've bottomed out at 10 below.
A jungle of snow is vining up
the day. Night falls, ritual and fast.

3.

Even dreams are static. The frozen womb
you crawl into each night holds you
as fast as amber the arachnid's legs.
Promethean to the night, you count
the links in chains, wonder at what
secret you can possibly possess.

4.

Sounds you hear hang in old doorways
like the severed lips of liars, false
to the last bitter bite of that cold steel.
The sharp midwinter wind cuts a steady moan,
one you ride on across the reluctant moon.

Autobiography, Chapter 2: Setting Out

The green blurs across your eyes. It is May, you remember, and you are leaving at last. Oklahoma! The window of the bus you look out of throws your shadow into the trees: even the shadow is green. You try to save your face. You swear you'll be a seasoned tenderfoot.

The land swells and rolls, then spreads out like the night toward Oklahoma City, where you know you'll change for El Paso and the Southwest to cross the desert Coronado knew all the way to an ocean you cannot yet dream. You will eat the desert and the high loneliness of the buttes: this is your dream, the going. You will consume the land; it will course your veins. You will be in and of the land.

The City, widest town on earth, is barely limited by the arch of sky. Miles there is nothing but neon and hard sin. The City hits your face with the smell of hot tar, an acid eating at your eyes. Two infernal hours and you leave, frightened and glad the Greyhound cuts the night clean as lightning. Too many ghosts are loping at your heels, but you know you are running straight to what you were born for.

Into the night, dead night now, finally free of neon and breaking shadows, you feel yourself flowing on some river you can't yet name, but it does not matter. What matters is that you know you are going and the going is good.

The Exact Center of the World

The owl among the trees screaming
like a mad mother's ghost is gone.
The mound of the guarding owl has sunk,
its skull nearly level with the ground.
The stones move in. A new forest
in twisted form crawls to the place
you found hard midnight at fifteen:
heard the screech owl scream, the moon fall,
and the breaking of ancestral bones.

Here you knew a first real fear and ran
past the second wind you never felt.
Dark times. But now the moon is back
and your eyes clear in the chalk of night.
Now you know all the ghosts are dead,
except the one never laid to rest:
this mound in this clearing is the exact
center of the world. All things move round
it. And here sundown explains nothing.

Against Metempsychosis &c.

Now that I am old and uneasy under the weathering trees
    and see time in the light of the fog
snaking among branches, hollows, low places in the earth,
the days slough off themselves and from themselves and all disease
is a floundering of the mind to comprehend at last the first
    rule of rot: that the melding logs

underfoot are hostel and hotel for claw, fang, tooth, nail.
    And yet I cannot see the rhyme
at the end of the log, the metrics that make the ebb and flow
of wood flesh turn fowl or field right in the diffused pale
aura of each winding day. That days should ever snow
    themselves green with a riddling mime

is not to be I know. Thanks to the wobbling earth seasons
    hold: gnats bite, die, things work out. What
I do see is little more than ant, a refusal to mourn
something I can never accept, a passing. Few reasons,
and fewer still, do me now that I am old, stiff as horn,
    untidy, subject to bugs, their snouts

always out. I'm unreasonable clay. I will not change nor see
    beauty in anything as obscene as
a passing day. Age, easily attainable, sees me now
flounder, fish out of water, in a world (forever knee-
deep at least) of slip not of my making but mine, and though
    fired through with a mind as flaked as

vintage pots, I'm lucky to make mud pies in this slow time
    that anyone will believe in,
much less flaunt with praise. Of course I am much bothered by loss:
insipid verse I can't recall, taxes paid, a traffic fine,
a wife, two kids in school who can't do math, or dental floss
    biting in my gums. All this, then

some nut comes philosophizing on rot, the great skein of life.
    Just what I need certainly is not
a dissertation on rot. Give me the bad mind that boils
in anger against rot, fever between the eyes, tempered knife
blade in the temple. In short, mine. Little though it is, it coils,
    will spring, be sprung (who cares?), not rot.

Autobiography, Chapter 19: For Andrew Grossbardt, in Memoriam

The slow summer falls about us like manna, sustenance
> we do not understand. The August moon wanes toward
> harvest here in the heavy heart of America, where
> once you timed your words.

Abstractions warp my tongue: I taste hot iron whenever
> I try to reason why *that* last act. My thirst was
> yours, yours mine, you taught me that. Now in this
> quiet time I lean toward the night to try to hear
> the echoes of a song, music you lived by, words
> and words alone.

Whatever siren's call you heard before you leaped into
> the storied night, my friend, is your last once
> upon a time. You must have fathomed deep, tied
> as you were to words, to loose the bounds we all laid
> round you daily and unaware.

The silence that is your death I do not take lightly.
> It passes as the wind passes, as the rays of the
> sun shimmer into the sea, as the seasons endlessly
> roll round earth—with circumstance.

Autobiography, Chapter 4: The Mirage

Out of Yuma and heading west, you feel the lift of air: a thermal dares you to try your wings.

There is a dance of heat way down the road, a swaying atmosphere, and suddenly you see the dance turn clear as ice, and above the ice a mountain that is not there.

A floating island and a cold inland sea: too much for the mind to take in such a heat. You bat your eyes and caves of wind take form. The island undulates in dance. You think you see a ship.

The desert dips, and your mind is slow to follow your body down. Heading toward the end of sky, the bus realizes the road. You see the mirage with another set of eyes. You see the mountain real as the wind against the window you count your own eyes in.

Wild Horse Hollow

The sound of drums is the distance
in your ears. Stones swell these hills,
and the hogbacks hunker under the honing
moon as if the land fears a deadly siege
of night. The moon turns your hands
gunmetal gray: the muzzle of your wrist
begins to glow, and why you came grows
vague under a shooting star. You stoop
to taste the snowy earth and night
you know you'll never be able to dream.
A sudden shadow strafes your eyes.
You flinch, and your quick finger
triggers into the forked stick you hold.
The wild horses you swear you know once
were here have left no sign, not one
trail across stone to hang a legend on.

Autobiography, Chapter 5: Ghost Town

Boards the shape of shadows, windows blued by the awful
    sun, the black hollow of gone doors, and always the
    constant sound of wind.

You try to take this absent town in one bound of soul,
    afraid you'll stumble on the derelict years only
    the headstones name.

You fail. The mind finds a stop: a rainbow in broken
    glass, a stream of dust in the washed-out street,
    footsteps you can't possibly hear.

The half saloon bangs its half a door the wind walks
    through. Night falls like hail, down with the
    thirsting hills.

You spread your blankets before the blank eyes of the
    town and lie in wait, a poor thief, for the permanence
    of stars. Inside your throat hangs a silence: there
    are no words, no words.

Autobiography, Chapter 8: At the Sand Fields

Sand shifts under your feet as though it flows toward some silent,
    dangerous sea: sand, weeds, and an ebb and flow of a sun
    that flails your back red.

A lone hawk circles high, a question of territory in his sharp cry;
    a desolation burns at the marrow of your bones.

You have pirated these fields of artifacts for as long as you can
    remember, but the numbered bones have yet to make a man, or
    even yet a single limb.

You have not learned the hawk's song.

Still you run the swells of these fields looking for survivors,
    the perfect stone, the last jigsaw bone.

The hawk cries again, and the sky flags piece by piece down into
    your face, and your eyes crack with the sound of broken weeds.

Loving the Distant Nude

She is lying freely among the dunes,
her breasts, her thighs, slow and undulating,
like the oceanic swells beyond the dunes.

The subtle flesh and the rise and fall of dunes
rebuff all fact and logic of the day:
I mold my own body into the dunes.

The distance is growing dark between the dunes.
Her perfect thighs are wedded to the secret
night I place us in. The air brushes the dunes:

flaws dissolve in the black and white the dunes
become in full-moon light. Distant, we are
engaged in an act of love, like dunes on dunes;

distant, yet wholly one, each knowing the dunes
hold the other's eyes, the other's body.
The touch is more real, the distance bridged by dunes.

The Family Plot

They tried to get me, one and all,
to go to church, sit in the front-row
pew, pray. I feigned indifference to
God and man. Oh, secretly though
I was awed by the graveyard through
which I ran when moon and owl

both were dark and I late for home.
Only the lateness of the hour
made me a boy brave enough then
to take the shortcut through flowers,
stone slabs of unacknowledged sin,
the *Requiescat in Pace* blown

in the unrelenting wind. I knew
the stones that lined the path by heart,
not by head, and was struck, changed
by windy death each time the start
of night bird or stalking beast ranged
up the length of spine and through

my hair. Dead uncles, aunts, deacons,
all spelled death and I would have none
of that. Father, mother, brother,
sister, cousins, all woebegone
because they knew how much I'd rather
sing hillbilly than their true songs.

I hid my crazy fear of death
to all except the limbo souls
along the path I'd sometimes take:
only the shades could know my palms
were cold from more than cold, the ache
of aging in my living breath.

Tornado

I am running; it is night,
I run toward the light.

Dark cuts through me like whiskey.

The light comes from the house.

The house is running; it is still night.
The house runs toward the light.

Dark cuts through the house like whiskey.

The light comes from me.

Stopping on Kiamichi Mountain

Antlers ten miles. You read the sign shot full
of holes. Everything you see is at least
half lie. You gun the Mustang and the engine
pings. Bullets ricochet off your head.
Sulphur Spring the arrow points, and you stop
to learn again the canyon hard below
is home to snakes and tarantulas as fierce
as fire in jack pines.

               Nothing is what
it seems. The cliché clogs; you try to shift
your mind. You idle down the trail, half
aware there's little sign of game and the wind
is still. The spring is down, a trickle, crusted
with raw sulphur that smells of hell and crap.
The sound of thunder breaks the hills in half.
You had forgotten the deadly still is always
prelude to a wind that rattlers will even
leave their skins to flee.

                 The thunder jars
you hard into yourself, the land. The sound
of home. God knows you know the tornado's
wake will suck your sins right out your guts.
The trees shake in the first wave of the wind.
Darkness descends like a hawk on prey.

                      Antlers
and you'll find yourself in that other home
away from home. The Buckhorn and three-two

beer. You feel you've earned a drunk, one that
will cauterize your guts and put a handle
on the wind.

        You head the Mustang straight into
the dark and pray the only times you ever
do that you know the wind by Indian name.

Autobiography, Chapter 42: Three Days in Louisville

> Everything is the cause of itself.
> —Ralph Waldo Emerson

1.

Coming down into an air brown as whiskey, the plane
    drops onto the strip like a practiced crow ready
    for another's kill, talons wild for dead game.

This fierce town will hold you three days running:
    the nervous prance that cracks your bones tells
    you plain there's nothing sure about sure things.

You count your chances for survival slim; this is no
    town for poets: the weather is never right, the
    air a constant sour mash and scream.

The city sprawls like a gutted horse, and the taxi
    you take can't even offer tours, the hotel so
    cold it smells of juniper and gin.

In East St. Louis this morning a stable burned;
    the horses screaming in their stalls, a total
    loss; and now you burn, wild mares beating in
    your brain, but you're no hero, barely sane.

You will read your poems to whoever is there or to
    the night; you will read something with hoofs
    in it, something with hands, something in the
    saddle to ride mankind.

2.

You eat Italian with your friends, who have driven a thousand
 miles, weathered well through the gangstered middle of this
 land, are green for poetry and bourbon on the rocks.

The horses in your head are pulling at the reins, anxious for
 the race they cannot run; a heavy smell of char stings
 your eyes, the sight of steak singed and bloody turns
 you cold.

There is no muse to pull a poem out of this pot; your fat
 friend across your plate plays Petrarchian with his words,
 the bad sonnet falling from his mouth like sauce.

When you were young, the horses in the meadows danced
 and the grooming wind greened their eyes and the sun
 filled their hoofs with fire.

Now the horses die, die, and the violent sky cracks with
 the thunder of stampede, gods gone crazy in the whiskey dark.

Hands above your head to keep your vision clear, you rush
 the car, stagger in mid-air: half buried in the rainy
 pavement at your feet is a spent cartridge of a Smith
 and Wesson .45.

3.

The muraled walls are big with horses' heads; paddocks
 and colonels are cornering at every turn you make.

You enter the Poetry Room at half-lope, late, your bones
 popping like pistols at the track. Three days in
 Louisville and your brain ferments a race you swore
 you'd never see: you dream pasterns broken, nostrils
 flared, a bullet between the eyes.

You loose your poems and the words run out, but you can't
    loose the horses in your head: in Tennessee, or somewhere
    down from here, they wrap the pasterns tight in wire
    and the Walking Horse learns his name dancing three-
    quarter time.

You've come to dread the afterwards, the taking stock that
    follows poems that's supposed to help you tighten up
    the pace. You know it's hard to drop a line or life.
    Always too much at stake.

The bourbon you finally allow yourself in bed is pure flame.
    You take it like you take the lie of sunny weather on
    TV. Agape. On the nightstand a phonebook and a Gideon
    lie neck to neck.

Self-Portrait

I am
before
a window.

A rain falls,
a leaf falls.

Behind me
a door closes.

Autobiography: Last Chapter

Coming in again, you know the town by boards it makes eyes
    touch, summer shirtsleeves worn long, heavy hats pulled
    down.

Always the wind stinks.

The woman you loved summers ago sits pale as bleached stones,
    her husband mad, their house a heap of broken bones.

The sky lies faded denim above your cousin's store; the false-
    front from another age, dogeared as a tinhorn's wild
    joker, can't reflect your past in its cracked eye.

You want to cry, but know the sun turns tears to salt before
    they break from lids in this desperate town, where the
    only hope is a brittle Baptist bell banging sometimes
    Sundays.

You touch the woman by your side and want to explain the lack
    of paint away, but don't: she knows you are running back
    into yourself.

A Season of Loss

For Carolyn, with love

ONE
Bone Yard

A word has power in and of itself. It comes from nothing into sound and meaning; it gives origin to all things.
  —N. Scott Momaday, *The Way to Rainy Mountain*

Bone Yard

A hundred buffalo
knee-deep in sludge.

Bones bleached to pebbles
and white sand.

No buzzard troubles
now to drop an eye
on long-spent bones
at this dried waterhole.

The land's cracked hide
speaks of thirst.
No tree lives.

Only the ghosts of hoofs
that still tramp along
play on a hot wind
which has no past.

Only in dead of winter
do the hoofs grow still,
when humped clouds
crowd low against the ground.

Paiute Ponies

Silhouettes, they lean against a ringed moon,
their heads down against the threat of snow.
Below, a distant diesel moan runs
along the tracks, where dead coal cinders
gather frost, and plays out toward Winnemucca.

No movement. They hump against the night.
Only quivering patches of skin crack the air,
memories of a summer's fly.

Mane and tail hanging vertical as ice,
they sleep dead centuries,
or if ponies dream they dream.

Below on the flat where light strikes water,
a last ember sparks out. A dog complains.

The diesel warns again, begins its roar, passes.
They raise their heads like automatons, blink,
then drop once more into centuries or dreams.

La Plata, Missouri: Clear November Night

FOR DAGMAR NICK

Last night in La Plata an avalanche of stars
buried the town in constant light the way the red
coalburners on the Santa Fe used to send fires

climbing night and falling back again, burning sheds,
hay, carriages, whatever was set along the track.
An avalanche of stars, last night the Leonids

fired every farm with ancient light, curdled milk
in Amish churns, and sent dogs howling through field
and tangled wood. Never was there such a night like

this. Lovers sprang from one another's arms, reeled
away from lurching cars and thoughts into a state
of starry wonder no human act could have revealed.

As if by common will, house lights went out. The late
work left, families settled out into the snow
unaware of cold, unaware of all except that state

which held us all for those long moments. We saw
and saw again the falling stars course Bear and Swan,
take field and farm, take all, and give it back as though

a gift given was given once again. Our lawn
on earth was full of promise in the snowing light.
Earthbound, we knew our engine on a rare November run.

Halcyon Days

Charlie Wolf used to whittle skinning knives
and swords from empty apple crates in winter.
He carved out blades I knew would never break,
true blades I knew instead would slice right through

any weed I chose to make a running deer
or any Rhode Island Red I chose to see
as enemy of God and man. Each old hen
knew my whoop meant feathers lost or worse

and squawked accordingly. Old Charlie used
to say that's why we got so many eggs
double-yoked—"scared the stuff right out of them
with that sword and that wild-eyed Choctaw yell."

Every sword I ever had before Charlie
drowned drunk on a coon hunt on the Arkansas
smelled of apples. Streaking round the barnyard
junk like a bullsnake after chicks, I breathed

pure Christmas before each ambush of red hens,
the white pine sword gleaming between my teeth.

Near Crater Lake

Between hill and river the trail
forks, edges deep in stone only
shadows know, and only the stones
can say which way my fathers took.
Steps and lives have worn away
the mountain agates' chalky maps
so I can say they went this way
or that and knew the sounds upon
the land, knew too the rush of wings.
The hill fork leads to a sky beyond
the hill, the river fork down water
fast with rainbows and quick jacks.

Ways my fathers walked are things I
learn from hard stones. I lift my arms
and hold the bear, the bull, the lost
maidens, and the hunter mad for game;
I make a prayer for the drawn bow
to send beyond the sun and down
the last dark corridor of sky:
old fathers, when you come again,
old fathers, tell me once again
why the path forks and the river
runs fast with fish to homes beneath
another sky, homes beneath the sea.

Thunderstorm in a Nevada Ghost Town

The horses know a rain turns quick to flood
north of Winnemucca and shake their hides
in a leaky lean-to rattling in the wind.

The gulch that cuts the Cattleman's Paradi off
from what may once have been the madam's house
begins to run like lobo sin
straight to Yaqui Chihuahua.

My wife tells me there are bottles at the rear.
I watch a spider take a desert fly
too dry ever to have heard thunder.
Stained, deep purple bitters bottles:
she lines them on the ratty bar.

We came for relics, not the deep red water
we watch claim the morning's tumbleweeds
and spent lead from range war .45s.

The drink we take from canteens wrapped
in Hong Kong wool is Himalayan tea, we pretend.
We wait until the gulch goes by. Dry, we ride on.

A Rannaigheacht Ghairid on Spring Burning

        Slowly, smoke
settles in the hollows. Poke-
weed grays, cinquefoil withers, jack-
in-the-pulpits crack. Frogs croak.

        The woods ring
alive with the fire of spring.
Though the flame may kill first plants,
no rants are raised at burning.

        Rather now
in this cool time of hawk, owl,
and hummingbird—acceptance
of the balance due to fowl,

        beasts, creatures
of the leaves and grass. Features
of ash give way to the force
that will course fields and pastures

        with a green
that will outlast the first seen
things of the small woods and ways.
All the days of spring we keen

        being slow,
loss of faster things. We know
so little the force of fire:
death here, we say, should grow slow.

Song of I-see-o*

I have watched the changeless mountains receive the sun.
I have seen the prairies black with the trampling buffalo.
I have heard the wild, dark cries in winter's hungry wind.
I have tasted the sweet and flowing water of the Quohada plains.
These things I have done, and I am glad to be a man.

I have counted the ageless stars in the Moon of Falling Leaves.
I have sought in troubled dreams the other side of the sky.
I have lived to see the prophecies of Maman-ti come to pass.
I have known the hot anger of Satanta and Gui-pah-go.
I have ridden through the Moon of Going Geese with Tay-nay-angopte
And my heart rides on to Rainy Mountain, my heart rides on.

I have watched the changing prairies receive the sun,
And I remember plains where grass was tall as man.
I, Tahbone-mah, have lived the old ways and the new.
The loneliness of the plains, the boredom of adobe walls.
These things I have done, and I am glad to be a man.

No more shall I race through nights of the Big Leaves Moon.
Before the Moon of Buds is down my spirit will pass
From this my mouth and ascend to the Great Milky Way.
But my heart rides on to Rainy Mountain, my heart rides on.

---

*Born Tahbone-mah, later called I-see-o. Died March 11, 1927. Kiowa warrior and later army scout under General Scott. Keeper of one of the great Kiowa sacred medicines.

Maman-ti, Satanta (White Bear), Gui-pah-go (Lone Wolf), and Tay-nay-angopte (Kicking Bird) were Kiowa chiefs.

In the Days of Many Horses, for the Kiowas and Comanches, Rainy Mountain and Rainy Mountain Creek in southwestern Oklahoma were sacred and favorite camping places where the grass was always green and the buffalo plentiful.

In Memory of a Day Nobody Remembers: September 26, 1874*

Who is left to recall the sacred earth
where Poor Buffalo bit the dust?

The dance of days is the only dance.
Town Indians drunk on Chock and Thunderbird

can never know they were born of a hollow log
or the ritual of the sacred sun dance doll.

Nobody can recall the massacre
of men, and horses dead in Tule Creek.

The racial memory fades. O son of man,
what anvil hand forged your soul and skin?

Isatai, who promised to vomit bullets
at Adobe Walls, would have you dance again.

Or Maman-ti, who willed the death
of white-tongued Tay-nay-angopte.

Exploded bones fuse with sand. No grass grows.
Of the chinaberry trees, just one or two.

Palo Duro Canyon: echoes also fade.
K'ya-been's bones lie buried in the bluff.

Dance, ghosts, among the yellow leaves
before they turn to dust.

*On the night of the 26th, Colonel Mackenzie and his troops from Fort Sill attacked the camp of the last freedom-loving Kiowas and Comanches, killing Poor Buffalo and several others. No soldiers were lost. The next day, the cavalry slaughtered between 1,000 and 1,400 Indian horses near the mouth of Tule Creek.

January Wind

From the low
cracked clouds this clocking wind
turns the fresh snow stone

and lovers
to their beds where the cover drifts
like undulating dunes.

In this cold
time, wind is law, relentless force,
that you cannot coerce.

You judge
the wind by standards not your own:
reeling planets, the sun

falling out
of sight, even the long wobble
of the earth, its spindling pole.

Harbinger
of death and a stillness time cannot touch,
the wind does not instruct.

Nonetheless,
you feel that the January wind
knows the in and out of things.

At the Burn on the Oregon Coast

The hills' heads lie bodiless on the mist,
ghost ships deadlocked on a ghostly sea, masts

rigid and dark against the faint ashen light of dawn.
Among last trees, the ringed fingers of sun are slow to sound

the depths of gimcrack trunks. The flagged trail
wakes to the wayward gamming of jays. The last wail

of an owl sinks away: the night bird battens
down fast against the day. Now the running wind

wafts through the crossed bones of trees and beasts, quick
as needles to thread the hills together, to stitch away the dark.

On the Mountain

The hide is nailed
upon the door.

The old bitch strains,
licks a sore forepaw.

The pup trails asleep,
hounds a first
wild hunt into
his hell of dream.

A low wind
lifts the dust
up off the floor,
inches it
toward the fire.

The pup runs
a spastic course,
freezes and bays
himself half awake.

The wind dies down;
the fire sparks out.

The old bitch groans
herself to sleep.

The hide is nailed
upon the door.

Right Place, Wrong Time

> You have noticed that the truth comes into this world with two faces.
> —Black Elk, an Oglala Sioux

At Lame Johnny's hanging,
they say
one old left-over Sioux
got drunk
& started a racket heard
beyond Hermosa.

He sang & whooped a circle
round the tree
like some goddamned witch on holiday.

He prayed
in four directions, kissed the horsedunged earth,
counted clouds,
& summoned up his grandfathers' ghosts.

They say he sang
it to the world old Lame Johnny's one eye
got big as a buffalo's,
the other the size of a rat's.

He prayed
all day, while Lame Johnny danced,
& circled round & round
what they say he called the sacred tree.

Postcard from Poison Spider Creek, Wyoming

Dear wife, space is momentary to the mind,
someone nearly said or wrote. I cannot
remember poems. Road maps have webbed out words,
but the feel of landscape here makes shutters click
even at 70 plus. There's something strange
about other places makes you want to
get where you never have to be: that point
you marked at sunrise. You watch the purple
turn to brown and marvel that all the creeks
are dry. Mostly you are afraid to stop,
and if you do you look for what you know:
your eyes are cameras that filter out the real.

Trying to Hide Out on Rich Mountain

Ruins have raked this mountain down to bedrock.
There's a lizard here quick as lightning
in the creek. Unique. Alone. So too alone
once this castle's ruins. Restored. Don't litter.
One year's life the great inn had before it
fell like dusk when all the Dutchmen went away
praising Wilhelmina, the old queen, her rusting
bones. You are here in soberer times. The green
mountain reeks of rotting moss and fresh crap.

Forty years you've lied yourself a life,
and now the woman that you love this late
knows all the barstools in the state, knows them
as you know these turned stones torn ragged
by a Caterpillar's track. The day opens
on your hot cot. You think you've fooled her
with this phoney suicide. She knows you were born
to cry. A lizard on your foot burns you
with a stare. The day opens wide enough to love.

Weekend tourists out of Tulsa sing
their beer cans empty. Four more beers they'll gun
their heavy cars down to Hot Springs sauna bars
and hear hard rock about mountains they will
never have to climb. The day stays open.
Wide. Wide as all the skies your forebears watched
eagles in. You wonder if you'd know their kind.
But it's too hot to pray Indians out of stone.

Four Things Choctaw

1.

Nashoba. This my father taught
me how to sing: Wolf, I look long
for you—you know to hide your scrawn-
y hide behind the darkest wind.

2.

Isuba. Horse: not one less than
twenty hands and all fast as hounds
with foxes in their eyes and off.
Chahta isuba cheli.* Once
Choctaws bred horses not many
winds could catch. Listen: isuba
still races winter's darkest wind.

3.

Baii. Notice the oak, the high
white bark, the heavy leaves, how they
fall. Winters are long in mountains:
springs freeze at the source and wind bows baii.

*Fast Choctaw horse

4.

Abukbo. The feather that all
my life I sought beyond the sun.
I have fashioned a sacred shaft,
smoothed it red with wet clay and poke.
The feather will guide its arc down
skies where grandfathers walk the woods
quick with game, heavy with the wind's wild mint.

Choctaw Cemetery

Stones,
hand-hewn symbols
touching four winds.

Familiar glyphs:
*ushi holitopa.**
The dates:
short years.

Pollen settles
down on quickened stones,

and from the east
a distant roll of thunder.

---

*Beloved son

Rabbits

A single-shot .22
and steady hand
could make you king
among the beasts
or ashamed to face
the checkerplayers
who were too old
to beat the field.

You killed because
you loved it
still; they crowned
kings reluctantly,
spat between cracks.

You could not know
the checkerboard
held acres
and each move
was deadly as
a hollowpoint.

You shot rabbits
until you lifted
the last one by the ears
and found a brain
checked, crossed
with a thousand moves
a rabbit had to take.

Black Mesa Sundown

Clouds bruise
the hill beyond
a flint-strewn mound.

A painted sky
is best at red.

To count this sundown
you'll need more
than broken stones

and at your back you'll know
the icy moon and spinning stars.

Reading Santa Fe

Here the wind is a bad witch from the north:
beans and tumbling stones, sheep and hogans,
grip the earth when sand blasts adobe raw.
Leaving Santa Fe is no mean task. You
steel yourself against an afternoon of ease,
feeling a new grit forced into your guts.
The last pueblos know the wind better
than any tourist can.

                The museum
you came to see sits alone, saddling
the hill. Its hogan-dome inside climbs
to an apex you feel a star is raftered in,
a light for those who remember to look
up. Days are fierce within this wind
that spirals around the hill and through town.
There's something about the plaza that smells
of a gone and still unacknowledged sin.
The good Bishop lingers in the pink skin
of adobe walls.

                You hear spiders pray
as the wind touches bells that do not sound
and doors to the cathedral forever locked
against a night that's bound to arrive on time.
Hope lies in the absence of wind, in jambed
lives of tourists ogling nickel silver
and strings of plastic beads. Wally Whitedeer,
flat-assed and sweating under cameras,
counts dollar bills between gusts and reckons
he will buy that horse Samson Sorefoot tried
to gyp him on. That's his dream a weekend
in advance. Then the pueblos will ring with

horses hoofs and bells he'll put on the pommel.
Five dollars, he intones in Hopi drawl.
The tourists move along to Janey Feather's
belts. He'll lower his price on beads and smile
when the sun sinks into the softer earth
and the wind begins to lie.

      In the heart there is
a pounding. In the heart of Santa Fe
the drummer drums because he wants a dance
no one knows the steps to. His beat strikes
the clock above the plaza and minutes jump
off cracked hands the Tewas know mean exactly
nothing: the ultimate no one disavows
who draws this hard Mexican air.

       Mountainward,
the April snows begin to melt. Somewhere
the horses toss their manes and neigh into
the twilight of someone's ancient gods. In red
light the neon adds a gilded glare.

      Galeria
del Sol features *An Afternoon of Rest,*
a portrait of a reclining woman muffled
in her dress, and for a modest fortune
she is yours to hang beneath a cross. Why
you are here and about to leave is something
you cannot know when the wind is native.
Twice in nine months you arrive in Santa Fe;
twice you leave, with regret you cannot name.
You are here to read your work to faces
lined by wind and red earth. You do not know
the angles of this land nor what the wind
hides from the hands that have summoned you.

Black Mesa Nocturn

A last ember
sparks quick
and dies.

You hum, hum low,
to see
if the ground
is real.

The eagle-bone whistle
lies cold
about your neck.

You count the cold light
of a hundred stars.

And you know you'll sleep,
sleep.

Badlands Mirage

The sun against this butte
burns black earth back
to salt and slate

and ghosts of deer
track down from stars
brittle as spun glass.

Echoes in brilliant light
burst into being.

A buck bruises a pine
to velvet
where you know
no pine is

and does
are dozing
in its shade.

A Sunday Dreamer's Guide to Yarrow, Missouri

FOR BRIAN AND SHARON BEDARD

The town is tilted toward the stream,
oblique as shadows toward twilight.
But only the stream is on the move.
No wind to shake the rusty leaves
off trees that have never known a spring.

Standing on the bridge, you think the town
a creeper, some gray vine, thirsting
after a force to drive it home
into the hill.

        And on the hill
all the houses are asleep, or dead.
Rainbow Bread is basic metal now,
and Stamper Feeds has only ghosts
of gears. You want a flight of birds.

Yarrow was once a flowered town:
you think of mint. There is no one
to ask, no one to tell you now
where forebears lie.

        There are echoes
you are afraid to hear. You look
hard into the water and put a leaf
lightly against an eyelid to see
who is in your thoughts. A vision
dances on the skin: it is you,
the dancer and the dance.

        On the hill
a last fresh grave blooms prismatic
in its finality.

A Season of Loss

We left the horses in the draw
and climbed the painted ledge to see
the blue and distance home but saw
an autumn sun set fire to trees

on ridges we had yet to pass:
gnarled trees that burned and stood
more than a shifting phoenix, cast
in colors other than mild moods.

Our blood was now too thin to know
the half-moon brother, our skin too pale;
yet we, hands out, tried again to sow
our spirit in the stars. A frail

effort: our fathers' blood pulsed slow.
At our back a glyph grew perfect:
hard in stone a hand drew back to throw,
a sun stood still, a moon arced, sticks

grew into bones. Only human,
we touched thoughts, hands, eyes,
assured ourselves of the moment,
and leaned together hard against the sky.

A Song for All of Them

Hills where my father hid the bones
lie dark about me. I look for
trails hacked hard in trees and lined
in stones all years war with. I am
here this one night to find the farthest
corner of the sky, to place my body
one with earth, sky, to talk with ghosts
long silent, long dark. The turtle
is running through the tree, the flint
knife is shadow forced into stone,
the feathered snake holds hard in clay.
The way clear I can remember,
signs my father drew in the dust.
Hands know, hands talk. I salute the sky,
breathe quick hunters, slow bears, maidens
fleeing hard brothers and red shame.
Bones beneath my feet, I make
a song for all of them. My name,
earth name, is sacred as the sun.
My name goes with me out of this world.

A Season of Sun Dogs

For days you never see the sun,
always expect the worst. Double
or nothing. You write next of kin.
The sky is lead, and will not melt
even under a sun going
down double. The clouds hide stones;
the sun dog predicts a snowy
doom. Best to stay indoors and pray.
Word is out as far as the hills:
blizzard is much too mild a name.

You listen for the wind and try
your charms against the heavy north.
A voodoo doll might end the dread,
but north of Baton Rouge it wouldn't
work. The only hope is rain from
the Gulf, soft with the down of geese.
You send your soul away: say "take
it" to a friend who's heading south.
Cornfields as far as you can see
die flat under the weight of iron air.

A silent sun dog laps around
a cloud. You believe the two suns.
You have no choice. The ground beneath
your feet becomes another world,
one you know you don't know and can't.
You say a word, try to normalize
the lie. Nothing works, again. You
slit your eyes against the keening wind,
plan dirty jokes for cards, tell yourself
things change and hope the hell they do.

TWO

Dog Days

    L'ardeur en secret, l'adieu à la vérité, le silence de la dalle, le cri du poignardé, l'ensemble du repos glacé et des sentiments qui brûlent a été notre ensemble et la route du chien perplexe notre route.
  —Henri Michaux, *La Lettre*

    Hidden passion, farewell to truth, silence of the stone, scream of the stabbed man, all frozen dreams and burning emotions have been our lot, and the dog's road confounds our road.

Dog Days

I dread the sultry August when days get short
and shadows long creep out to the mountains of the east,
when the dance of heat is seen far down the road,
when rivers no longer run but squat like turtles in their scummy houses.

For it is then that the dog trails my shadow,
his swollen tongue dragging dust,
a growl hidden behind filmy eyes;
when I stop, he stops, half within my shadow;
when I move, he moves, in step.

I dread the sultry August when days get short
and the sun seems a ball of fire-froth,
slithering from the jaws of the rabid beast
of sulky summer days
and my shadow lengthens and the dog is there.

Rest Stop at Horse Thief Spring

The air is thin enough to make you cry
for home, and sounds among the cracking stones
ring of rattlers and long-dead horses' bones.
The military crossed here first, then horse
thieves walled the spring and stayed to build
a stone corral and die. A grave is opened
every year and all stones turned up for gold.
The laughter of dead mouths is keening in
the wind. Like waves, the thud of hoof on stone
never dies. A crow is drinking from the spring.

Three thousand feet above the valley's floor,
you caw the carnivore away and taste
his wild flight in water as old as sin
and cold as nights under this winter sky.
You hear the horses' breath, their frantic leap,
their rage to know the prairie far below.

Let them turn stones. Or tourists piss
in springs. Miles away from woman and sleep,
you know this sky is full, this earth alive
with sounds it will take you long days to hear.
You give five minutes more: to dream an ambush
and a hanging as heavy as this mountain's back.

Sweating It Out on Winding Stair Mountain

The roots around your soul and eyes
after too much bourbon twist sockets
sore. This mountain's too high to cry
sober on, the sky too wide to fill
a brain. Three crows are wheeling
up a peak. Caws crack thin air.
Sweat ices its way down your spine.

Last night love loomed as lonesome
as a timber wolf, the face a mask
you painted in your drunken dream.
What's real is that one white, brittle
moon you think you see pied against
the coldest blue a summer has known.

Nearly forty years and you've yet
to learn that love is measured by
the sun. There's no shade. The wind
pulls at your hair. The sky burns black
at sundown. You've got to go back down
before the crows laugh you straight to hell.

Return to the Roundup Tavern

FOR THE OREGONIANS

Broken neon lariat and aging horse and rider
still signal sundown to street and S P tracks.
Sign and tavernfront are naked as the memory
of last Sunday's whore in Klamath Falls.
The building sags like some swaybacked mare
once swollen with life but now a ruined hulk,
grazing between the S P and the Mercantile.
The asphalt shingles curl like dead oak leaves,
into themselves. A blacked window reflects
the sunset.

       Silence sits like oil outside
the tavern. The street is half holes; the S P
goes black at dusk. The boardwalk sinks, creaks
of nails in fir. I pause at the battered door.
Inside, a lone shuffleboard player aims
a puck. The bartender dreams a fold-out.
There's an acid smell of piss and old pitch.

Silent as time, ghosts form in the shadows:
Tex glued to his customary stool by the tap,
elbows rigid, snoose juice streaming.
Old Pete, dead under a runaway S P car,
stands mid-bar. Big Ike, crushed under
concrete, raises one finger as if the act
itself were creation. Ivan lies stoned
on the perpetual floor.

        The battered door
is cold against my hand as the lone shooter
releases the puck and the bartender goes down
on an invisible page.

        From the Wurlitzer:
dead voices of Williams and Reeves and Cline.

The Long Lone Nevada Night Highway

Strangers we were friends for a long moment
on that long lone Nevada night highway
at the wreck (two dead on blankets or carcoats
on the gasolined pavement under our stars,
one other palely directing non-existent
traffic). He from the south, I from the north:
the long Nevada night highway is like that.
We both set our front-rear flashers working
and dug lone flashlights from stacks of states
and helped the dead, but did little for the other
till the trooper arrived (someone came before
us; he was known to us; he had stood here).

It was not blood or hard black pavement that
finally shocked us. These are commonplace.
Nor was it twisted metal, death, nor survivor.
It was only this: that after the taking
of numbers, after the siren's wail, after
the sanding of blood and the sweeping of glass,
after the conjectures, the sighs, the regrets,
what would there be to hold us to this spot
on the lone Nevada night highway where the stars
blanketing earth were ours and we were one?

Dirge

Struck dumb by whispers
from the bed where I had
never been rocked, dumb from
my mother's return to him
from some far world, dumb from
her solid body not warming
the bed where we lay nightly
since I could remember arms,
save the forever she had been gone,
I heard their strange words.

In the wind-roofed loft above
my bed, rats rattled their quick
toes in that close tin hull
where night words went
to a final echoing rest.

Darkness surrounded me:
in my small vision, words
wasted in whisper rolled
like tiny scattered bearings
through the listing loft
no star shone on.
Words, silence, rats' feet:
the immense unending dark.

Somewhere beyond the reach of wind
I dreamed, dumb with knowing
she had come back to him,
that this beginning was the last
of something I could not name
in the vast inexactitude of youth.

In dull morning light
I woke to no memory of night, but
woke to the sounds of her slow step,
of wood and poker, of fire climbing
the tin stovepipe, and to her face
blue in the dawn room light
and the sheets trimmed and cool
against my cheek—and, O God,
it was something to be alive.

Decades

> Though nothing can bring back the hour
> Of splendor in the grass . . .
> —William Wordsworth

Then I never lost a song. Time was ever slow
and long. The grass flowed green to brown and back again
and I with it without reason except to sing
the silence full of sound the way the working wind
below the clouds found voice among the trees and low
of cattle grazing along the fence-rowed edge of field.

In my first decade the days bloomed wild with ravens
gamming brilliance, jays thieving, martins feeding quick
above our roof. There was no rain, no small neglect.
The immaculate skies did not portend a future storm.
All nights were warm, and innocence was there within
the house, the barn, the slow animals of our farm.

In my second decade I knew the war, of course,
which first loomed glorious, remote. Weapons I made
from empty apple crates. Then Time began to fade
into the shadows of my face: I could recall
yesterdays. My brother joined the Eighth Air Force.
I lost a dog. In those hard years, the first hard fall:

the weather taught me each could be the same—day,
love, war. Whatever I made a habit of
was deadly. And death did not end, only the brittle love
of first love I thought I'd not break through, then forgot
before the season turned. In that long, slow decade
I did not sing but flew the flag upon our lot.

In this whichever decade, my song comes slowly now,
the right sound seldom there, to catch Time where he is
or was and hold one moment in my hand, the chance
not guaranteed, but sought word on word, until
I hold a memory in light I'll surely know
and all the long loss of gone days is finally told.

Yuma: The Greyhound Depot

A turquoise sky
low enough
to rub.

One bird,
maybe hawk,
a wing of light.

Somewhere,
a dog barks
silver as the night.

The smell
of a sin you can't define
in wind.

Years later
you will remember
only these of Yuma,
and a sudden pebble
in your mouth
will grow wet
against any desert
you have to cross.

The Sentence

On my desk is a cup which is empty.
I drank the last of the tea only a few moments back.
The cup is empty I say.
I want the cup full.
There is nothing to do with an empty cup.
I look for a tea bag.
There is none.
So strong is desire that my eyes water.
No tea in the world.
All cups empty.
I have died for the want of lesser things.

Notes for a Love Letter from Mid-America

> There is no death. Only a change of worlds.
> —Chief Seattle

1.

No horizon promises a mountain.
Cornfields hide sparse trees
like snow the stone.

Mid-America in dead November
lies glacial
in the wake of this
a season come too soon.

I miss your eyes
in my eyes.
I miss my breath
in your hair.

A season of no promises
& a season of long regret:
we gave up our sense of place
for a sojourn in Mid-America
& you are gone in these
our elliptical days.

2.

We are happy in our mountains.
But roll them out
like unruled paper
& memory hangs like a pale woman
rocking on a wall.

Without a horizon
there is no land
worth the moment shared
when hills flung back
the best half of your name.

A sense of place
allowed us room to love.
No wonder salmon
take to falls.

I could die
where hills know
how to reach. Not here:
landscape will not allow
an *I protest*.

Wind breaks corn
that seldom sees the sun.

3.

Lost River. I remember it
by white-water sounds
& salmon mad with love
& rainbows dead,
rotting in the weir
my brothers made.

We swam the rapids
to love where moss
claimed rocks smooth with years.

You know the way it was all too well:
image is idea.
My eyes are full of you.

I will write runes
when letters fail.
For any part of you
that calls me fool
I'd give all mountains
I have left.

4.

But mountains do not last
where wind turns faces
hard as glacial drift.

Your name sinks
into the frozen offing

& only the taste
of crying it
hangs like an icicle
in my throat

& this alone I have left
from our sojourn in Mid-America.

Sundays

I cross the river, the solemn bed of moss, the song of water over rocks.
The choir sings above the river sounds.
The stones and the river listen and the moss on the thrown skulls of fish.
All words are soft this Sunday.
Let us cloister this choir and resolve the disputes of the lost.
I do not know how anyone feels about war.
The stained glass throws haloes onto the pews.
The cross is falling, with all this light.
I am falling, falling into another solemn approach to the altar,
    that perpetrator of cold deeds.
I know still water runs deep over the dead skulls of fish, turtle, drowned man.
I alone listen to the choir of orphans.
Moss grows cold on the dark bark of trees and the detritus of night banks.
I can see the bottom of the shoal from the last pew and feel the presence of
    fishes and loaves.
The river confesses to the wind.
Only the fish listen through their one window to this other world.

For Geoffrey Firmin, in Hell

> ¿Le qusta este jardin?
> ¿Que est suyo?
> ¡Evite que sus hijos lo destruyan!
> —Malcolm Lowry, *Under the Volcano*

Below the garden on the hill
the barranca cuts through the road
and at the bottom lies a dog
rotting among old cars and dung
and grotesque masks from festivals
and traces of the Consul's bones.

And they have weathered long, these bones,
whose house had once loved well the hill,
loved well the fun of festivals,
and had at last walked down the road
to Parián with a sad red dog
to take his place among the dung.

Nothing now except bones and dung
remain to tell the tale; the bones
were not ferried across by the dog,
across the stream and up the hill,
but lie beneath the hill and road
amid Mictlan's dark festivals.

Tourists attending festivals
have often looked down at the dung,
while pausing whitely on the road,
and often wondered at the bones
but never guessed beneath the hill
a man was slaughtered, and a dog.

How horrible that reddish dog
then haunting Firmin's festivals,
constantly howling on the hill,
smelling of pulque and of dung.
A sack of skin with shivering bones,
it ate its puke upon the road.

And slanting down the Parián road,
the Consul sensed the shadowing dog
and felt the dread of death in bones
too tired for fear or festivals
above the barranca and dung
below the garden on the hill.

Now up the road I see a dog
and look beyond the bones and dung
to the festivals below the hill.

Odyssey

1. Dream

My father moves out of the dark
and touches me.
I sink away.

Bring light, he says.
There's something outside.

I push myself up on elbows,
full of dream.

I go through all rooms.
There is no light.

There's something outside, he says.
Hurry.

I go out without light
into liquid dark.

He is not there.
Nothing is there.

2. To See the Sea

On the way we encounter storm.
The springy heather is leaden, gray.

The sea is over the hill, he says.
We're almost there.
                Night falls.

The crows are silent, hidden.
Only the wind . . .

And then the great gray mound of water
backed by cloud . . .
There, he says, there is destiny.

My infinitesimal eyes strain against infinity.
I cannot see.
I hold tight to him against the wind
as the rain comes down.

3. Requiem

An aroma of wild mint.
People sing to flowers.
Brave boy, a hand on my shoulder speaks.

—Dust to dust,

The horses are bathing in the sea, my father says.
You will not see that often in this lifetime.

ashes to ashes.

The roses are wilted.
A dandelion bends beneath white stone.

Don't look at the sun.
It will put out your eyes—like that.

He is laid to rest.
Pray for his eternal soul.

Walk carefully into the night.
Let your eyes grow used to it.

A lone bird streaks skyward.
My eyes follow it.
The strange hand bites the bone of my shoulder.

Surviving the Storm

The night the lights went out all hell broke loose:
a swirl of ghosts blew every other fuse,
the television burst, forecasted fate
rode wind and rain into another state
and left us sitting staring into the space
where all those years we'd fallen out of grace.

We watched the night as never before we had
as if something in the liquid dark were mad
and we were in for it, whatever the clouds
and balled lightning, furious roofs, and shrouds
of untreed birds could hurl our way. We prayed
into the brilliant dark as rafters buckled

like the deck on a rotting ship where doom
rode mast, bow, and souls of sailors gone dumb
with fear of falling into a maelstrom wide
as any Baptist view of hell. The side
of the house catching the brunt of wind bowed in
to the breaking point and snapped back again.

We smelled the hail. We felt something tornadic
in our joints. The roar of a billion bricks
breaking through took our ears. We could not speak,
nor did we dare to try. We knew the break
in wind would not come before our skulls cracked
and we descended breathless, damned by the black

sky, the relentless force that had willed this
all. We told ourselves we would never guess
that such a thing could hit, could dump us from
our chairs as easy as wind a feather or frond.
What mattered most was that the landscape freeze.
For that, and that alone, we bit our knees.

Certain death did not come. The hammering fist
pulled back, and the bellowing night grew still as mist
on moors. We unhinged our suppliants' limbs
as if they were fragile doors on ancient tombs.
We spoke to the night. We reconciled our fears
and with open hands reached for the light of stars.

Autobiography, Chapter 10: Circus in the Blood

My father's blood is strong: my bones grow hard with
    stakes in things and my veins pulse with a lively
    red from his nomadic ways.

There's a circus in my blood I've waited forty years
    to know, my father's hollow glance weighing on
    my shoulders like a sledge, his eyes gone blank
    under the sagging tent in dog days.

So here in this nonesuch bigtop in slow August, I
    surprise myself into a certain knowing. This
    thing is in the blood: a lust forever to move
    from place to place perfecting the one best act.

Henceforth I swear I will delight when I can name the
    earth new under my feet, keep my eyes clowned on
    where I am, and juggle my thoughts fast enough
    not to bore my ears.

And I will try to know the dancing in my blood, how
    it reels, steps, stops, and how on occasion it
    swings me out of tune, a dizzy fool whose brains
    are slower than his feet.

And I will praise my father for his shifting the shape of
    ways, for letting me know the permanence only of
    road; will praise my father and swing my heavy
    hammer to guy this my own ephemeral sky.

On Location at Tongue River

Half a town has grown
where you shot Goodman Two Cow
off his boulder horse
and started an uprising
you were Custer in.

You feel it's right
two slumping, feathered bucks
on painted pintos
cross the street

and the movie company man
grooms his beard with water
from a rusty turnip can.

You always knew they'd find
this place and make it
what it wasn't.

The scene grows stiff,
then dissolves into the game
you always played.

Who shoots first don't make a damn:
the important thing is falling.

The pintos reel away
and two bucks lie
giggling in the dust.

Crow

A crow calls from the ridge. Twice. Three times. I pinch my nose gently, cupping my left hand over the bridge of my nose. I caw the way the sawmillers taught me. I am a fool to think I can fool the crow. I caw. Twice. Three times. I see the black wings settle softly in on limbs high above my head. I never knew it would come to this. How I continue the conversation is exactly the point in question. Like an idiot, I put my hands in my pockets and stretch my arms with senseless glee. The crow preens his feathers, gives me sidewise looks. He drops like lead to eye level. The low limb twangs. I can see the world behind me in his black pupils.

The Drowning

     From the rock
she dived into the shadow of herself,
        and, hurling

     the surface
into rainbows, her form split the mirror
        of all forms,

     and some god
held her long, too long for breath once held.
        Her lover

     woke slowly
into death's dream, calling as one might call
        another

     at dawn to
wake into a day in which each vista, distant,
        is flooded

     with first light.
She did not return, her fair form held deep
        down below.

     Her lover
moaned, endured, and still the water
        held her form.

     We could not
free her from the slow shadows that she palely
        quite became.

>   Though we tried
> our eyes and skill, nothing came up with our breath
>   but a faint
>
>   taste of lilies
> and our curses against the play of light and shadow
>   down among
>
>   the gripping
> depths that held her silent, still, and we turned
>   our curses
>
>   on ourselves,
> and, as the water blazed us back odd voices, our eyes
>   chiseled at
>
>   every stone.

Heartland

The houses die, and will not die.
The force of walls remains. Take
the family portrait hanging oval
on the wall and, underneath it
on the chifforobe, a dish of mints.

There are houses that fall, but their
shadows stay, lightly against a summer's
dusk. And there are photographs that
show ghosts of mothers walking halls,
of fathers fiddling in moonlight.

Even in disrepair, there's a life
to the houses. The rush of wind stirs
a soul: footfalls on wood and stone,
the creak of kitchen door, the last
words of a son gone away to war.

The houses die, and do not die.
There is something that will not let
a space be given solely to grass.
The aura holds, the center will
not fold, forever framed against
the graying sky, the coming night.

Ghost Fog

> I heard an Indian singing behind a rock pile. I stopped and looked. It was Poor Buffalo. He said that it was a great honor to be killed by an enemy, and that K'ya-been already was asleep.
> — Mumsukawa, a Comanche

At false dawn a dirty fog rolled up through
my camp on Tule Creek. On the first low wave
rode the heavy smell of a prairie dog town.
Then with full flood tide surging into the mesh
of my sleeping bag came earth-born, sky-bound
smoke of ancient campfires: Palo Duro Canyon:
the trill of an eagle-bone whistle, summoning,
the flap of a sacred owl-skin shaken high,
and Maman-ti's prophecies from the shadow world.
All stuck to me like red Texas mud. I dared
not move. I had scratched for horned obsidian
among K'ya-been's bones high up the canyon wall,
and the spidery hole moaned deep, forbidding,
and those webbed sockets branded me *Neuma-taker.**
The sun had made me brave.

                                             But now in this
dark dawn I thought I knew how it had been:
hunted, there they had still been free to choose
a place to die, to choose a place to die.
A hundred years flowed back and I was there:
Poor Buffalo has gone to sleep, his mother said,
my life is broken. And she wailed, wailed.
Shadow world.

                                    Then out of the pitch black west
a low and rumbling thunder set me straight.
Here was now: a trucker, damn his tunneled eyes,
barrelling-ass down the Amarillo-Lubbock run.

*"Eater of human flesh," a Comanche term of contempt for Tonkawas.

The Captive Stone

AT HEAVENER, OKLAHOMA

Enmeshed in steel stands a stone,
near stunted ash and elm, cracked bones
of Yggdrasil, small trees of time:
the caged stone with ciphered runes
is part of Park where men once made
their mark with maul and biting bronze.

The aged stone, hard to hand's touch
when touch was still allowed,
has had its face forced clean:
lichen lies dead below washed runes;
webbed shadows of encircling steel
now mark time on the lone stone;
yet the stone stands as stone stood
when Odin still was king and came
with men to mark down lives and fates.

Now we who Sundays look long
on this stone's stark ruined face
see only stone and ciphered runes
under the steel's sharp shadows:
the whispering of wind through wire
carries scant legend, no hint of history.

Parable

Like a midnight eye, the hollow moon
opens wide against the empty jar.
The drumming light falls on leaves, on stones,
on the woman in white beginning to fill
the jar.

The hollow moon is laying down
a plan still a long way off.
The light that falls is all around
the woman and the jar. The woods are
enough

for the woman at the jar, and the moon
is enough. Its hollow light fronds
the trees like a summer storm. And soon
the woman will have filled the jar
and gone.

And the moon will have dropped into and beyond
the trees all its drumming light, full
and moving, a stratagem that dawn
throws no light on. After the moon, only
a lull.

Accident at Three Mile Island

> how everything turns away
> Quite leisurely
> —W. H. Auden

The island steams under the opening sky.
All around the narrow length of land
the river flows as it always has, and late

birds heading north to Canada notice
nothing unusual about the air.
There may, or may not, have been a disaster

among the undergrowth: what birds may tell
is augured late at best, and fish homing
upstream are mainly interested in falls.

Who knows? At any rate the land was calm.
Nothing surprised farmers off their tractors
or knocked the rheumy cattle off their hoofs,

though something surely must disappear every
time the earth shakes or the sky moves an inch
or two to right or left. Still there will always

be a boy fishing from some river bank
who doesn't especially want anything to happen
except summer and a dog scratching at his side.

Toy Soldiers

During the war
we drew all our troops to us.

We reveled in our reality
of wrong, marched miles across

littered plains, bridged chasms
hell could not imagine.

There was an art
to our displacement of men.

We leveled towns.
Territory was our game;

to take and hold,
our order and our last command.

Too small,
we could not think a Buchenwald:

not once
did we save one Jew.

Now forty odd years past,
I go back to that scored hill of dirt,

taking our whole battleground
in three strides—

the fortifications barely discernible,
the roads merely passable.

What scars we left
grow invisible:

the turbulent grass
is climbing toward the light,

though at the roots
I hear a drumming of small lost things.

The Pawnbroker Takes Final Inventory

Mostly I recall that blue bust of him
she hugged into my shop before they took
her off, though I remember, other times,
the odd anguish in her face as she held
on to her man's gone arm at this counter,
his drunken logger's idiocies branding
him fool the rest of his short staggered days.

Cancer took him and ravaged her insane.
Duty to the ghost of that poor woman
holds back all indecencies. What matter
the battered kids and broken rosary?
What I remember most is I knew she
suffered and loved, true to her deep devotion
to the fool. She pawned that blue legacy, too.
I gave her what I thought I could, and more.

I don't sleep well. Heart, you know. I knew him
when art failed him, or he his art. Who knows
genius? He bragged about his work in fir
and hemlock. And sold none. Winters he said
he burned his best work to stay alive. I
have hated myself, mea culpa, many
a night: I often see that simple piece
she painted blue. Don't ask why. I'm ashamed
to have taken her last token of his art.

Now, surely, somewhere in the green reaches
of loggerdoom, her mad sculptor unlimps
and lugs his chainsaw deep into timber,
decking a tall heaven full of angels
and grace. There in blue light she waits, his stew
steaming over pitch, coffee in the pot.

I've kept it out of greed: I longed to hold
what was left of the poor art and artist,
something I'd never get from the watches,
music boxes, old coats, lies. I have it
here, under the tarp, the odd and the end.
It is yours. Consider the clarity
of pain, the total blue. You may wish to
remove the paint. It is permissible.
I know the wood is blue: it must be blue.

Call It Going with the Sun

Where Fourche Maline runs into Holson Creek,
first it almost does then backs off and makes
a circle so that an almost island
sits as though the river's god forgot his job.
Corn was growing on the hump when I was too
young to gnaw an ear. Now it has faded
back to forest, or just about: river
birches stand thick as cockleburs once choked
corn. It smells of musk and old earth where I
kick a last food's log and turn up a black
twoheaded stone axe and a gunning sound of quail.
I'm too vague to care: my head is too full
of generalities. I cannot think
this a field of corn. How can I reach
Caddoes or pre-Columbians said to
have lived this land? I came to fish but think
of paying rent, the way it has to be.
I take the axe, just in case it charges
me with the fire it may have felt.

                        The line
hangs straight into the stream and bends. A minute
on my butt and I drift. The current's vague.
After rent then what's left? That blonde I saw
the other day showed me my age: cold fish
eye. Why I came back I will never know.
Fox squirrels killed here have no grave where I
can kneel, and bass never bite when the sign
is in the groin. Call it a try at going
with the sun.

       I tell the wife I want to get
away: a needed rest. But not from her,
I lie. Going I know I'm free, but that's
another lie. Earth never is the same.
I remember cornfields, but find a forest
and an axe. The field once I ran across,
lister rows thick with river grass: here is
another world. One I don't know and don't
care to. My work is with the real. But how
to live? I make mine eight to five and see
the joke. A stone axe in my hand is cold
comfort. Crumbling, it's hardly worth the trip.

5-Ring Circus at Season's End

(CARSON & BARNES)

The artists are tired, tired: the sky has fallen
from their faces. A triple turns into
a flop. Even the net is slow in rebound.
The flyers' arc lacks the majesty of apes.
The catcalls of wild children rip the tent.

Clowns out of round empty their buckets on
rows one and two. No one flinches at
confetti: the trick is slower than the mind.
No one wants balloons that will not rise or
cotton candy elephants have disclaimed.

The cats refuse the flaming loops. The tamer
cracks his slow whip on empty air: the lions
will not wake, and the toothless tiger chews
a wrong memory of home. Not one cat couchant
or fierce enough to open the midget's mouth.

The jugglers lose their pins. Knees buckle
on the wire: the drop, a deadly 3-foot-6.
The spinner cannot spin by teeth alone
and begs the spectators to let her have
her hands, hung heavy with the brass of rings.

And now the grand promenade. The brilliant flash
of tights and eyes is gone. The heavy weight
of hoofs, a precise funeral march, brings all
performers down to earth, their final show,
to bow at last in a dangerous company of beasts.

La Plata Cantata

For the memory of my mother and father,
Bessie Vernon Adams Barnes and Austin Oscar Barnes

Gill Netting the Beaver Pond

1. Packing

Strange to think after so many years
that I worried about what to take
fishing overnight up Holson Creek.
It seemed I was leaving on a journey
I had my doubts about. But an odd
sadness made me see the washed out
road leading through the hills without

the many ruts and rocks. I did not
know how deep a night was. I took
too little food and a quilt I would
not use. I remember that I thought
of storm, of being taken under
by some monster in deep water
while we defied rain and thunder

to stretch our net through the shadows
of trees on the pond. I did not pack
one fear intentionally: I acted
the twelve-year-old I surely was,
hoisted the duffel up on my
back, and marched to cadence like
a good scout should before he dies.

2. The Netting

We had heard stories of big bass,
lunkers wallowing like grown hogs
in the old beaver pond near the bog
where cottonmouths parted the grass
at night. My brother knew his way
in woods and water and I stayed
close on his heels at the end of day

after we had set the gill net.
The sun had fallen red into
the timberline, and the pond grew
immense before the lingering heat
turned chill. The quiet flap of bream
we thought tangled in the net seemed
a portent of a bounteous stream.

At midnight we ran the net. No
bass, no bream, but half a dozen
eels squirming, crying their human
cries, and their soft round faces so
full of pain I could not hold them
in my weak sand-coated hands. A dim
moon rose. We skinned and gutted them.

I knew I could not eat their flesh,
but morning woke a hunger in
my head, and I ate what I had been
in the deep night in a dream of fish
when I had hung limp, by the gills,
tangled in a web of threads no eel
could mistake for Sargasso swells.

3. Driving Home

No matter where I looked the low
mountains were waves on some blue sea
I'd lost my way in. At my feet,
on the floorboard in a wet toe-
sack, six other eels lay in the slime
of their only defense. Low limbs
clutched at the windshield as we climbed

up the rutted road that led home.
The motor made a steady whir,
and I thought of cold spinning stars,
for a reason I cannot fathom,
unless my mind had taken on
some migrant trait not everyone
would want to trouble with. The sun

somehow was still setting as red
as the evening before, and the high
thin stars began to offer light
webs across the sky as we reached
home. I felt myself suddenly caught
at twelve by a motion I could not
stop: I swam in the night like a moth.

Surveying near Ellsworth, Kansas

All that's left is hard,
the bone-dry creek,
the knife shade of a single tree,
the prairie burned brown by a screaming summer sun,
and a lone marker,
stone, belonging god-knows-where:
scalped 1853.

The Heavener Runes

Old words vague
as reeds on water.

Gouged runes
cold as glaciers.

Who can tell
a thought
from stone?
Only the glyph
speaks.
Thought is lost.

The thing itself
remains.

Hot earth.
Cold sky.
You between.

To make a mark
you become the mark.
Your name.
A woman's.
The date.

It does not matter:
you are the mark,
you are the stone.

Near Cimarron, New Mexico

The wind you can never face,
heavy enough to bruise an eagle's back,
whips cactus bare as bone.
The only sundown that you can believe
in is a lone horseman
racing across the plain
toward everything that he owns
and nothing that is his.

Great Plains Tornado

Thirty miles away
it stands still,
a pillar of sky,
dark with the antiquity
of Roman coins,
shattered mosaics.
Byzantine.

Fluted stone,
joints of lead
somewhere always
crash and fall
on a prairie acropolis
and strew for states
artifacts hammered
to useless seed.

South Willamette Valley Bars: A Memoir

Goshen

Many an exile
has done time
in the Goshen Bar,
suspended
between home
and the promised land.

Eugene

The Oasis
stands just off
the main drag,
home for confirmed drunks
and would-be sheiks of Araby.
Here hot air is constant
in the liquid Oregon night.

The Sahara Club,
its sands run out,
hides behind a new facade,
the genteel Eugene Carriage Trade,
dress code rigidly upheld. Once
you didn't have to drop your jeans
to enter here.

Springfield

The Driftwood
catches the dregs
of the mighty Mackenzie
and drunks who were only always
passing through.

Creswell

The Roundup—
rocking rider
and broken neon lariat—
longs for the good old days
when honest drunks
knew how to dance, how to ride
the voluptuous woman
behind the bar.

Cottage Grove

The Dog House,
pointers and *setters* at the rear,
is sanctuary for hunters and loggers
and two lovers gunned forever down.
The wallpaper: buckshot and blood,
the pride of Cottage Grove.

Circus Poster

With lion couchant
below
and tiger couchant
above

the blue rainbow
spells
your eyes,

arches over
rearing horse and whipping
rider,

her tights
wondrous
O,

and two clowns
all mouths
sighing

the white air
that fills
the ballooned words.

Once in Winnemucca

Eating soggy bean sprouts
in Winnemucca, Nevada, at dusk
after a hard day's drive
was poor tribute to the opium tin
I'd kicked out of Jakeleg's mine.

Stringy things, fried by a red-haired Swede
who said he herded sheep in winter.
My rockhound summer was ending under
the blue light of plastic lanterns.
Through the wall I heard a jackpot ring.

I wondered how a Chinaman felt
in Winnemucca's snows and what the tin
had in common with a sweating Swede.

The lanterns "made in Ft. Smith, Ark."
gave off an opiated glow.
I hitched my sagging Levi Strausses
about my hips and left the frying
Swede without a tip.

Stations

Texaco
(trust
your
car)
reeks
(to
a star)
to high
heaven

Shell
(sans
s)
connotes
sea

Deep Rock
promises
(a
cool
death)

Phillips 66 (6)
(power
to
give
life
unto
the
image
of
the
beast)

Flying A
(ultimate
re-
ward)

Dreams the Children Had

The fall the circus did not come
was gloom only the children understand.
The weather was mad: the owls went
screaming through the trees, and some

lone dog was always barking on
a leash. Nights elephants traipsed
the sky, their trumpets sounding depths
of the children's dreams, and Bongo

the midget grew a giant, his stilts
booting across oceanic beds,
and now and then a muffled dread
swelled the waves in the children's quilts.

But the children slept, and less aware
of world: their clouds rolled, billowed into
a spangled tent of night and through
symmetrical rings of mind and air.

The children's eyes grew perfect, round
in sleep. They sang to the calliope,
danced the perfect rings, and then the
dangerous beasts laid themselves down

even at the children's feet. The first
fear they may have ever had was gone.
This was their world, their true home,
and stars splayed down upon the earth.

Icons

FOR SAM RAY

1. Hand

Imprint of a hand.
On the stone
when the stone
was soft. The perfect
hand of a child,
the lifeline clear.
A hand outside time.
You see but do not see.
Take this hand.
The aura around the tips
of the fingers stays.
Here. Forever. Where
there was a hand
a hand still is.
Hand beyond a hand.
Meaning beyond meaning.
Meaning.

2. Gaps

The birdmen. Some
would say thunderbirds.
Only the glyphs speak.
There is no thunder.
The mind bends to seize
the stone. The image
is unchanging. The mind
closes too many gaps.
Open. The gaps
must stay open.

The birdmen hold
the stone. There
is a force I cannot
name. This force on
and in the stone.
Obviously, I cannot
even name the stone.

3. Icons

Time does not exist
except as a corridor
through which I pass.
There is no going back.
But the speed at which
I proceed is not constant.
Nor is the speed with which
I perceive. Moments in
the mind need icons
to identify the contours
of space. There is more
to be learned of the past
than will ever meet the eye.
I have forgotten more
than I will ever know.

4. Nape

Sight has weight,
substance, is matter.
Lucretius early knew.
Consider the back
of my neck. I will
turn to greet you
eye to eye.
Friend.

5. Room

Images of the past
dwell in each house.
Foundations.
I need a room
of my own so that
I can meet myself
every time I return.

6. Tonight Somewhere

For the first time
I see Venus balanced
on the sharp horn
of the scythic moon.
Not star within the
nether tip, but star
at swordpoint. There
are wars we have
forgotten. My god!
for the first time.
Tonight somewhere
on a vast desert
a pillar of fire
will amaze small
creatures, and they
will wait on elbows
for nothing
like understanding.

Something in the Blood

Blue Mountain. I know it
by the pines: knotty green
and sick on turpentine.
Deer camps fill thin air
with the smell of gutted does.

A return after months
of mountains of other sorts
to find a drunken ranger
squatting by the spring.
His right. And mine to drink:
the iron-cold water hones my blood.

This is home: we all come back
to kill. Something in the blood.
The bucks know and head due north
to the Fourche Maline, water
still stinking of Frenchmen
somebody's forebears killed.

I check the action of the 30–30,
slide hand-primed cartridges home.
A fox squirrel leaps limb to limb,
eying the elk-horn sights.
The finger tenses, eases off.
It's something in the blood.

Trying to Read the Glyphs

A hundred feet straight up this cliff's dead face
some hand chiseled glyphs. Abstract and open
to every sundown. To read these riddled runes
I have to chew the wind from caves I can
never know. Somehow the glyphs are right, in
this cold stone no glacier has ever kissed.
I expect a foothold, a niche to level on,
a ledge some wild lover knew before the leap,
but find only stone vertical as split ice.

A thousand years dead, the waterfall pours
dry fire into my eyes. The acid of
my sweat grooves the painted face fingers
claw into. The eyes reject my touch as I
pull the glyph to me like a departing lover.
I am body for the etched face I cannot
read. Flesh and stone, my mind is full of bones
the caves hide in webs thick as arctic snow.

Below, the river that I long for now
inches past, like a glacier hunting for
the sea. The shadow of a lone hawk spins.
Images of what I love fall with the sun,
and night brings me down, both shoulders sore
with bones I never knew I was heir to.

Postcard from Blue Finger Lake

At a cove on Blue Finger Lake I pitched camp,
hurrying to get the explorer up
before the promised shower soaked me through.

My wife's pale face kept haunting canvas corners:
she had not smiled at my weekend madness,
but had shaken her head, whispered something vague.

The rain beat down on the flapping tent, then stopped,
which was also promised. I looked over
the lake's water being pelted, far out;

and then I breathed a somewhat purer air.
Dear wife (I envisioned a postcard showing what
she'd missed), would you believe there was a rain-

bow over the tent? I miss you. No, I don't.

Learning Balance

I coasted downhill before I ever learned
to ride the bicycle my father traded
the crazy blaze-faced mare for. I yearned

for more that summer than the quilted shade
my mother and cousins shared the gossip
in. I swore I'd learn to ride the shaky

thing. On first fall I smashed my lower lip,
broke two spokes and the fence into which I slid.
I tried again and felt all August slip

beneath my toes. *Learn balance first*, he said.
I took him at his word and used my feet
as ballast, sailed down the meadow hill ahead

of running cows and barking dogs. The heat
that summer turned fierce, and I turned twelve,
the wind and sun stripping my face in sheets

you'd swear some copperhead had just sloughed off.
I rode and woke into that different age,
one I found I could pedal through myself

with a fair amount of ease, without the rage
of innocence beating at my dusty heels.
That first bike, that hot summer, was a gauge

by which, my father knew, I'd begin to feel
the motion, if not the music, of this sphere
and claim my part as reinventor of the wheel.

Going after the Milch Cow

Always in the back pasture, the white-faced cow
never came no matter how long I tried to blow
her in, the horn so hard against my lips my teeth
felt as if they were bending like old nails under
stress. For several long years we milked that dumb beast
that would not come in to the sound of the horn. Her

udder almost dragging earth, she wouldn't move at all
unless you walked behind and whistled all the while
you gently waved her home. The other barnyard stock
were quick to trough, but the white-faced cow chewed one
slow cud: I never saw her swallow. Once a flock
of starlings roosted on her back. She left them on

all night before she slowly whipped them off without
any effort except her tail. I wondered how
you could make a slow cow go, how to get her home
in time to get the milking done by dark. I tried
all the neighbors said. Nothing worked. I wasn't dumb
at twelve; *experimental*, I like to think. I cried

a lot, but cows are used to bawling calves and kids.
Nothing ever seemed to work: she hardly shook her hide
to keep the flies at bay. The pies she left in that
slow wake I skipped till my feet were raw. Then I swore
I'd speed her up. I grabbed her tail and cranked the fat
rump like a Model A. I found her forward gear.

Touching the Rattlesnake

The neighbor's leg was black from toe to thigh,
with yellow pus oozing from cuts he'd made
trying to stop the poison from reaching
his heart. He showed the three of us stumbling
into his house, after Sunday school set
us free, what he said we would be afraid
to see. The swollen blackness made me shudder
with adolescent sins I knew we were doomed
to hell for. He dared us to touch the leg.

Tight as the shell of a dried gourd, the skin
seemed to break with each slight movement he made.
I left with the smell of venom in my lungs,
my eyes careful with every rock we passed
on the way to the swimming hole. I lay
on the shoal and felt the current crawl along
my body until all thoughts of fangs were washed
away and the rattle of leaves above my head
seemed only leaves. *Amazing grace, how sweet*

I sang straight up into the Sunday sky.
The others splashed my face, and we wallowed
like carp in the mud. We could not know that one
of us would die before the sun went down, fangs
buried in his neck as he reached over a boulder
to pull himself up the face of the cliff above
the swimming hole. Nor that he would live just
long enough to climb back down, boasting that
he touched the snake before it struck his neck.

The neighbor did not die, but thrived on guts
he said it took to have a snaky leg.
I could not forget the oozing blackness
and never crossed his door again, nor how
white the naked body of my friend lay.
The wind rose late that day and made the limbs
crash above our heads. That night it rained.
The sound of thunder and shotguns carried us
through a domain of snakes we would annihilate.

Hunting Winding Stair Mountain

The sky overcast, a threat of thunder
murmuring up the heavy south kept us
from hearing the trailing hound until the rush
of wind our way told that he had treed more

than we had set out to find on that day.
The forest of oaks and knotty pines obscured
even more the hazed sun we thought we had
a bearing on. I knew the dog would die

if the three coons decided he was no
real threat. With one shot my father took
the smallest one. Climbing, the others shook
with rage across the canopy of low

pines. I know we did not hunt for the sport
of it. I long ago forgave my father
for whatever sin it was that I swore
we were being punished for when we heard

the lightning strike the tree the dog still barked
up. The silence that followed filling the woods
I can't remember feeling since. We could
not find our way under the impending dark

that kept us from keeping the mountain at
our backs. The rain pelted us with some fierce
determination. We did not know north
from south, east from west, up from down, nor that

night was yet hours away. When the sky did
lift, the mountain loomed upon us like the storm.
We had not known it lay so close to home
that we could be halfway up the darker side

waiting for the moon or sun to take us down.
The old dog smelled of burning sulphur all
the way down the steep slopes on our slow heels,
his eyes surprised still by the god of coons.

First Cavalry: Holson Valley Road, 1942

The column passed on a slow Sunday—
cannons, half-tracks, and silent men
olive-green in the valley sun.
Before the dust of its passing

had settled I saddled the roan
and holding a gallop followed tracks
as far as daylight still allowed.
Dusk fell like a dare a long way

from the bivouac. I did not turn
back until I heard the mountain
lion. I reined the roan into
a full retreat: his flanks were foam

before we reached the barnyard gate.
Loser of a lesser war, I felt
my hair bristle at the wild cat's cry
and then my father's stern "Dismount!"

The War over Holson Valley

Across the mountain somewhere lay Texas,
where all the warplanes were migrating to.
Day after day they crossed the valley low
and humped to miss Winding Stair that blocked
the southern sky. You knew nothing of radar
then, nor that Texas from Dangerfield to
El Paso was a vast training ground for
Air Force personnel.

                     The valley knew the war
mainly from the thunder of heavy bombers,
the silver engines of fighters echoing on.
Forty years and you remember clearly
the P-38's twin fuselages barely above
the trees behind the barn, the slow milk cows
bellowing into stampede, their milk turning
bitter as gall. The radio gave you news
of the theatres of war, and you wondered
about the language of it all.

                     And now it
roars back, the innocence you were guilty of,
the guilt for years of playing war with friends,
who later left the slow valley for the quick
world, their Purple Hearts boxed among other
souvenirs. You knew it wrong to like the war,
its mystery of leathered men and wild machines.
Still, you imitated flight, with whittled planes
in the canopy of oaks and pines on the slopes
of Winding Stair. Wind took your hair by night,
and you crashed in fierce resolve, waiting
for morning's resurrection in pure air.

Bombardier

1. Bathing in Lethe

He came back broader, taller, than I had
remembered, his duffel full of wonders
he gave to me: compass, model B-17,
medals, ribbons, and silver wings. What's more
he made his aviator's cap fit my head.

For two green months that short summer we fished
the mountain creek across the open fields
our father plowed throughout the war. The bass
we caught he insisted we throw back, to
keep the stream alive he said. I wondered

why we walked the banks to try the deep pools
or shoals and why at dusk each day he stripped
and bathed so reverently in the spring-fed
stream while I thrashed about, torpedoing
a convoy of minnows or a frog. Now

I see I missed the mark. We bathed at home
with regularity. But the stream was
more than bath, more than an instrument
of cleanliness. The water sang a way
to be; the wind on ripples mapped our lives

with contours we couldn't see. Then my brother
was gone. The daily drone of planes from Tinker
Field told me he was gone again to war,
though in my mind I knew him bathing still
in a cool stream that washed most worry away.

2. Souvenirs

A hundred pictures of the London Blitz
or more he sent back, the postcards a pale
sepia and held together with Red Cross
gauze. When he wrote, the V-letter came crushed
by many hands, through many lands. Once
even it bore a postmark from Morocco

and a stamp from Roma. We never knew where
he was nor how. He sent an Iron Cross
from a base somewhere near Brussels in '45.
Just before the end, he sent me another
B-17 someone had whittled out
of Black Forest pine, its metal props

snipped out of a prewar tobacco can.
My mother loved the Irish linen. My
sisters gasped at the wonders that he sent
them, little things that made the marvelous
seem true. We placed the souvenirs along
the mantel and window sills and read his words

about a wider world he was going to help
us see. The war filled us with dread, so too
the age into which we grew. It was his way
to give us hope, the souvenirs, mementos
of being there, wherever it may have been
before he disappeared over the Netherlands.

3. MIA

The letters did not stop, and packages
periodically arrived for months after
the telegram. We knew the mail was slow,
but with fixed minds we saw him alive still
somewhere over there above the clouds bound
for places he would send us pieces of.

And then all stopped, and we began to think
of death camps that, before, we doubted ever
were, of how he might have glided in—to
crash into the walls to make a gate through which
the suffering could flee or simply to just be
there passing out mementos of the world.

No word ever came that he was found, nor
has it come. Forty-odd years and still I
feel him in the air, hear the sputter of
dying props that do not die, but whir on
into the dreams I have of this my life
that is also his life. Somewhere along

the lines of blood, it must be clearly written
we will not forget to honor the poetry
that daily then shaped those lives: the lost children
of the holocaust singing through open flames,
the welcome home for those who stood it all,
the bombardier still on his one last run.

4. Threads

Through the maze of years, I have stumbled on
too many tokens strewn about like bones
and have seen too little of the world I
think he meant to light. In the receding
sounds of planes flying far above his lost

domain, it is not just my fading brother
I sense the loss of. Something else drums
into the void, something once so big I
knew it would never end. I'd like the past
always flooding back: a river, a sea,

a soothing mist of atmosphere. I thought
I would remember roads we walked, the way
back after the setting out, the open doors.
Artifacts I hoped were private now belong
to others. I see them in the houses of

strangers, or gutted in windows of pawnshops,
their bright mystery tarnished by hard hands
that cast them away to live. Somewhere there
must be threads to piece together, threads
leading back to that simple complex time.

The Submarine in the Park between the Muskogee Toll Road and the Arkansas River

Gunmetal gray and salt with years
the submarine strains
toward the toll.

I never stop in all that passing.
Nobody does. Flags
on the conning tower

all always the same:
storm and squall.
But the wind's

a constant cheat.
Deadlocked belly deep
in red sand,

the boat is prey
to birds and Air Guard trainer jets.
Across the 4-lane,

half a world away,
the bartender knows
the North Atlantic

a pool of icy puke,
a lone Indian speaks
in an unknown tongue,

and two whores remember the war
they wore flags in
and swear

they'll blow this town
when the sky wakes up red
and their ship comes in.

Memories of Oceanside

The dark jetty
and one dead shark, mouth gone white
against the sea.
A flood of images
incoherent as the California sun
and you are back 30 years,
pollution, that biblical word, not
reinvented yet, in wide screen.

The boardwalk
and a few small honest booths.
You shot arrows at balloons,
an innocence at noon,
after your first long swim
in languid waves, the tar balls
a mystery of the deep.

Nights
of knives and bad dreams.
Appendix out, right flank scarred
and netted tight with dissolving gut,
you dreamed your fame
came applauded by the squawk of gulls,
a forethought no vision could quite hold.

Anchors
into this inland sea.
Here in these late times
you know only
sharks plastic and fulltoothed
above the waning pinball machines,
your good ghosts ebbing
slowly, slowly, like all sand,
down into the hollow night
where the fool is silent
and the clown forgets his nose.

The Game

The mad dog barked because he had to bark
at the dangerous shadows leaping toward his eyes:
we pulled his chain and clamored up the oak

in a fine delicious fear of teeth as sharp
as the spikes of stars spinning atop the trees.
The mad dog barked because he had to bark

at threats he defined as cruelty at the throat.
Oh, those were the nights we could win any prize:
we pulled his chain and clamored up the oak,

his nose objecting to our heels, his joke
not quite the same as our own, but surely close.
The mad dog barked because he had to bark

and play the game his captors chose, but spoke
his words his way, a merry rage set loose:
we pulled his chain and clamored up the oak.

We loved that fierce beast and the deadly stroke
his paws gave our dogged legs and skinned knees.
The mad dog barked because he had to bark:
we pulled his chain and clamored up the oak.

Ubi Sunt

Things were larger then and vaster,
full of wonder that would register.
When you go back again for good
to where you best remember you stood—
amazing and true, the philosophers'
sight! Frogs, weeds, and gophers'
holes, you seldom even notice.
How small, now, the wild oat is.
There's a shrinkage that overcomes,
vanishes ants and clover bums,
deflates skies, stunts trees, fences,
and generally assassinates our senses.
O, but we must wash the whole world
in explanational blather and swirl
all essence that is not pure or plain
right down the heady sewer main,
or else the dirt piles high again
and mountains grow and comes the wind
whipped by ravens' wings and magic
rules as once we knew it did. Tragic
that education makes us bigger,
moves finger from nose to hair trigger.

Night Letter to the Secretary of the Interior

In brown silence
the cheat grass falls
to its light task
below Spirit Mountain.
A spreading brown
is taking the hills,
and the mountain
will drop its green
before the salmon
make one last run.
Here at the center
of our last world,
we try to tell you
it is wrong to take
away the trees, to
let the cheat grass
claim the sinking
hills and stones
tumble from their
source. A smothering
earth cannot breathe
without the hair
of branches and eagles
in unbending wind.
Spirit Mountain
we will hold
when all else
is broken by your
will and odd way
of suicide. Only
a few now we
are growing daily.
Soon we will stand

before you like
a forest of legs
to trample your
floors as soft as
the virgin earth
was before you
sent the yellow
Cats and screaming
saws and dishonest
drunks, whose eyes,
white putrid flesh,
we stared down
Saturdays in town.
You will know us
though it will
be too late
for parley or
compromise. We
were seduced
to make us late
in moving from
ancestral perches.
But we have moved.
Beware.
Expect us soon.

Domain

The hawk sweeps in on a wing of the sun,
breaks to a stop, trembling and still,
like a skater at the perilous edge of ice
breathing a silent strength. Until

he places me in his domain
there is no movement of wind, talons
as rigid as old pitch around
the branch, the eyes steady as stone.

Then, only then, does he fall
into sundown, his eyes pointed
as swords, into the stand of spruce,
into some lair, through its dark heart,

down the hollow of the windfall night.

Day on day I walk these woods
and never hear a sound. Then from
nowhere: the terrible beating of wings,
the panicked cry, the toppling home.

This domain I walk carefully in,
aware of the eyes that pierce, the hand
that fells. It is not my place to
speak, nor the place where I began,

and I will not take from the hawk
the beating wing, from the prey the one
last cry, the sun its wing of light.
Only: I count my fears here, down,

down the hollow of the windfall night.

Paraglyphs

Two fish,
definitely carp,
picassoed in stone:
Holiday, Missouri.
In certain light,
flesh scales
under lichen.
Hot stones hiss
into the water pot.
There is a song
to the night moon
and to fish.
This cave, this mouth.
There are echoes
still.

—⚡—

This arc of moon, this scythe,
burnt by the light of eyes
into savannah sandstone.
What's lost concerns me
more than what may be.
A collector of old nests.
This arc of moon, this scythe.
Overhead a hawk, a shining.

—⚡—

The red ochre snake
may be seen in two lights.
A snake, horizontal, long,
sunning, recumbent.
The life of a man, the valleys,
the peaks, the slopes

and rising of the eyes.
And one other: enemy of heels,
brother of bonds,
the vein of life
I flow into and through.

———

I am a survivor of the sea
I do not understand.
Even the turtle,
that intrepid wanderer,
is better equipped than I,
a road map on his back.

———

On the banks of Holson Creek,
a short half mile from where
it joins the Fourche Maline
in silent flow to wind
farther east to the Poteau,
I found on the surface
of the rutted earth, after
a hard spring rain, 3 finely
worked arrowheads, 1 rough
spearhead, 1 broken adze,
2 pieces of thin clay pot,
and 1 large fragment of
a human shinbone. I call
this spot the Place of Acorns.
The white oaks along the banks
of the rivers bear fruit
the size of your fist.
A wholesome food, pure
protein, when leached.

———

Flying over Big Sur,
I think of Miller.
Houses hanging in
ravines, lovers

copulating in doorways.
The civilizing gray
and heavy air. All
tropics are rooted here.
Manifest destiny rainbowed
in radical dream,
and nowhere to go.

Cuzco:
the hitching place of the sun.
The sun stood still
on anchored and fitted stones.
And the earth stood still
in its socket of sky.

Three Songs from a Texas Oilfield

The cardinal drills
the brilliant dawn,
his cry as sharp
as a diamond edge.

—⚍—

The jay does not call
thief! thief!
Cousin to the crow,
he objects to darkness:
this bright land is his:
fief! fief!

—⚍—

In pecking order
the flicker is king
of ground and trunk:
dressed in black tie
and hammered yellow vest,
he speaks with the authority
of a pile driver.

At 39: *The View from Sycamore Tower*

To climb this shaky thing I came
too many miles and from a woman
I could have been drinking bourbon
with. The view is blue for forty
miles every direction except
west, where Buffalo Mountain humps
hard against the sun, its tower
making this one a derelict.
Map and triangulator long gone,
the lookout's table is runestone
for adolescent loves and relics
of the master race. The valley hard
below and north is now scrub oak
or sparse pine where I stepped barefoot
on my first rattlesnake, and saw
a naked neighbor chasing heifers
through the woods. I knew his life was
running out his deaf ears and he
out of himself. I knew fear for
dead days and could not look him full
in the face on Sundays when he led
the valley's only choir. The river
is blue as sky, the way it touches
nearly every house, then snakes
along a field and hides in trees
beyond the ridge. Running water
and running lives from this distance
are hardly more than blue ripples
in wind. The air is rare, chock-full
of ghosts and insects, and home
is always ten thousand miles away.

Below the Sans Bois Mountain

The buck had come down the draw in silence,
so quietly that in my stand I did
not know he stood in shadows of the pines
until the sun began to break the edge

of the mountain into splinters of light.
Then I saw him from my perch on the rocks
just above his head. My camera was not right
to catch him in any kind of decent shot.

Two hours before the false dawn I had dragged
my sleep-filled body up the mountainside
and set my lens toward where the mountain sagged,
waiting in half-sleep for the midsummer sky

to open on the rim. His eyes were fixed
toward the Sans Bois as if he, too, would take
something of the sun if it were given. Sticks,
stones, the broken ridges began to fade

into the light they were made of. The solstice
opened in ribbons of sky and cloud, a bourn
I would record on film, while the buck licked dust
and rubbed the bloody velvet from his horns.

In Hugo Country

A snowbound Crow smokes
beside a stove fired red with pitch
and counts white buffalo
cracking on the barroom wall.

The sky is sharp at 20 below;
the landscape always backed
by a mountain you never want to climb.
You learn the Flathead on your right
drove piles in Venezuela. Or stormed Iwo.

Sometimes you predict the weather
wrong and never hear a song for months.
You've got to be around a while
to know the land is real
and how to love under a ton of blankets
when the stove turns back to blue.

Horsefly, B.C.

Tired of climbing schist
and hard heights
of honey trees,
the last bear moved
to Banff for kicks
and Hershey Bars.

Tourists think it odd
that anyone could love
and die in Horsefly, B.C.,
and with their chisels
break away the names.

Those fading houses
flanked by scree
say welcome
to any soul or wind
the mountains send
to Horsefly, B.C.

Once there was a man
from Horsefly, B.C.,
came down to Calgary
for the Stampede,
never went back—
think of it—ever
to Horsefly, B.C.

Crossing the Kiamichis Again

Each trip in time becomes the same.
It's hard to remember separately.
I am driving across again.
The mailboxes have aged.
But still I see your name,
by the stone where it should be.
Now in this full dawn,
sentences of light strike the road,
and I read what I can
before the dance of heat
erases your good words
and the shouldering pines
grow dark under the raucous crows.
Day is breaking this time,
and I am still driving for Texas
and another sky I'll never find.

La Plata Cantata

1. Turkey Season

In early morning light you see them rise
from the branches, give their feathers a shake,
and drop gently down to the ground, their cries

scraping through the woods to herald daybreak.
You must hold still, black as the trunks around
you: no movement at all, nor eyelid tick.

In all the stalks the absolute you've found
is just this: not stealth, savvy, camouflage,
but your mind's immersion in the will of dawn.

These birds you hunt know more than swale and ridge
or weather rising fierce in the sudden south.
On days when your luck runs along the ledge

in easy shot, you count the lives in both
light and dark, the sum total of your frames.
What you take away from these woods and off

the land is spirit you hold in trust. Names
of birds and beasts erupting like wild dill
upon your tongue say that you did not tame

one wild thing, nor cause the low sky to spill
its rose or blue. Your camera holds a way
to be, and you another through your will.

2. The Palace Cafe

We sit here with our backs to the wall and drink
to all the things we should have done before
Armageddon fell upon this town. We think

we know it well, the mountainous cloud that bore
the very soul away, its winds whipping
roofs away, walls. It took the wives we swore

to God we'd love forever, honor, and sing
the seasons to. And took our sons. And then
our farms. There was total nothing on the wing

but cloud and wind. If we are lucky when
the waitress comes, coffee in hand, she might
say a word that will take our minds up wind

from this stinking town, what's left of it.
But we do not know it well: the changing sky
does not allow forecast. The winds that hit

us in the back that day filled the blank eyes
on the square with debris. The Palace lost
its shade, the window and a rack of pies

gone without a trace. The tornado cost
the Sabre Jet a wing, the park its trees
and tulips that survived the last hard frost.

With all the loss you'd think we'd want to leave
the state. We stay with nothing like we want,
save the Palace where we don't have to serve.

3. Bandstand

When I was just a boy, I crawled down
from my Red Flyer and under the old
bandstand, which was warping even then round

the edges of the floor. You could not know
what wind and wonder had moved to that dark.
I tell you there were mysteries that now

seem stranger still than all I knew to stalk
my nights. The bandstand was hideout for Huck
and Tom, pure heaven for the local pack

of budding musicians, den for dogs. No luck
is what we had: killer bees established hives,
they said. Now look at this stone block that took

an hour to pour, a bandstand with no give
underfoot, and underneath—no love. They
sold the old one to Hutterites. I believe

it's now a floor to a communal barn, hay
hiding lost bad notes and my honeyed sin
written on dark joists. So the sidemen play

and the leader sways on crumbling concrete in
all the festival we have. I say here
it's not the same: we need the darkling wind

beneath to lift the music from the fear
of remaining horns. From this stone kiosk
we cannot know the music of our sphere,

cannot know the beauty of arabesques
graved in wood, nor the tap of heels beneath
trombone and flute, nor the darker humming risk.

4. The Water Tower

Below the *Class of 86* fading
whitely above the winded catwalk boards,
two lovers strain to hear the same old song

they have heard radioed each night before,
since the song began and they, as lovers,
chose the moon as anthem. Under the water

tower, the light of the low moon covers
the song, stills the whispering voices that hold
the wind at bay, stills doers and movers

even in the town at large. The lovers fold
into themselves satisfied with the night
under the water tower, where the bold

hand has written its destiny in light
script and fading paint. Stark against the out-
lined sky, the tower claims its stilted right

to be the fountainhead of love and doubt,
billboard of fame, sentinel of a jerk-
water town, four-legged moon long gone out.

5. The Santa Fe Depot

The sun sinks into the westering tracks where
they come together in a thin steel line.
The sky turns molten and consumes the earth

at the low line of trees where fields begin.
Another day, another day, the old
reverberating phrase tolls against a wind

that rattles bones in this low place and folds
the past in a book you can't read. *Another day,*
the farmer's words for what he does not hold,

and for what he does. To stand here and wait
for the westbound train, you'd think the depot
had a life beyond the little lives that date

the hill: hues of sundown begin to flow,
and the cracked walls take fire. Shadows and lines
mark the station's empty seats. What you know

now means less than what this moment is in time:
another day, another day you have stood
here or anywhere to be counted in time.

6. Behind the Lumberyard

We used to slip into the lumberyard
at noon to smoke before the stack of two-
by-fours caught fire and they put up a barbed

wire fence six strands above our heads to do
what nothing else had done. We eyed the fence
and shied back into jimson weeds and blue-

grass gone to seed among the larks and wrens.
Before the big storm took the lumber piles
up into the blinding dark, I told my friends

I'd bet they'd never find us here, not while
the school year lasted. Our science teacher
did, plastic sack in hand and an odd smile

across his face, later, one day after
school. He stuffed the bag of long thin leaves
into a pocket and broke into laughter

we could not see a reason for. Toward the
end of summer he was gone. By that day
we all were hooked on Lucky Strikes but free

from the oozy knowledge that he could say
something to our folks we knew well to hide
or lose so much it'd take our breath away.

7. The Light above the Store

The grocer never blew out the light upstairs
until his wife committed suicide.
Why he let it burn when kerosene was scarce

no one could say, though I knew she was mad
before the English had left Picardy.
Sometimes through the window I saw her clad

only in a gossamer gown, herself ghostly
in the soft lamplight, from where I stood below
those few nights during that last liberty

after Pearl. When I came back from Iwo
less a man, the shrapnel wounds were slow to heal,
and she was madder still, the sickness so

severe she danced naked across the field
beyond the water tower before her man
covered her with a ragged quilt he held,

running, like a flag. I was there again
below the window when she screamed *oh God,
take me*, and nothing came except the rain

that forced me in. The night she took the drug,
he left. I was there a silent witness,
my eyes blurring against the coming fog.

Time was never right for that peculiar loss.
Nights, still, I think I see her there, wavering,
outlined by a globed flame in the gathering frost.

8. Savage Country

No one stands seven feet tall in La Plata,
not since Dent (alias Robeson) wrote
the Man of Bronze into the pulps, the data

wrong but Doc Savage right in a world not
to be ignored. Gone by 1959
Dent and Savage had saved their world from rot

and this town for posterity. But dime
magazines shelved forever under glass
can't keep the park alive, nor bring back fame

once it's faded through death's door as it has
here, where nobody knows Doc's name. The band
in the park is seldom musical. No mass

of blooms on the sad square will ever stand
over anything for long. The growing season
is short so far north, and the city hands

no longer serve the finer arts, the reason
given always the same: winter potholes
must first be filled and work on streets begun.

The town has grown as practical as moles:
all movement is toward greater things that sate
the sense of hunger of lesser human souls

than Savage and his cohorts had. The fate
of this Missouri town is wreathed on our
front doors, and what we know we learn too late.

9. Heavy Metal

My sign is Cancer, but that can never mean
I have to live under an ordinance
that would shut my mouth till the water's clean.

I don't think we should leave our health to chance,
not when our cancer death-rate is so high.
I told you when I ran I'd take this stance:

to admit our mistakes and rectify
the sin of heavy silence held too long.
We need to stop this useless talk and try

to set things right: admit the report's not wrong,
close the city lake, forbid the sale of
fish. The presence of heavy metal has hung

about us in the mist rising from the bog
each night and in the crawling things at water's
edge. All the children that have died, their dogs,

the cattle — let us say that something matters
more than the festival and tourist buck.
We've got to call the experts now to gather

samples once more of everything from shuck
to fin. Our grave mistakes are resting on
the hill. Let our stony silence have struck

its last blow. This has not been a good town
to believe in. Perhaps it will toward the end
when we can say we did all that could be done.

10. Urn Burial

When the elevator blew its top and fire-
balls shot a hundred feet into the air,
no one expected much of a loss. The gyre

of smoke was blacker than should have appeared,
though there was but little concern. Firemen
contained the blaze at noon, the 4-H fair

hardly delayed two hours, the parade in
progress before the church bells chimed at one.
The wheat was totally destroyed within

the larger bin, and the soybeans had gone
bad because of water damage. Insurance
made the owner smile at his telephone.

But then the sad thought came. Across the fence
the Chief had stretched to keep the children safe,
the wind stirred a mound of wheat. The chance

that anything could have been alive may have
caused us to count heads: one hired hand now lost.
We clambered up the remaining walls to save

our honor in sight of God and the First
National Bank. We knew him dead. Of course,
he'd caused the fire by lighting up. The burst

of light that caught his final act to force
him into what must have seemed a tall sea
of grain is one a simple oiler of doors

and dust fans could not know even if he
did survive, which he did not. We disinterred
his seared and suffocated form, while the

remaining walls circled us like an absurd
urn we could never dig out of, not in
this town even with the help of our lord.

11. The Annual Soybean Festival

It's the same old song we heard this time last year
when the lead guitar got sick and couldn't hide
it behind the mayor's daughter in her

coronation gown. The music always slides
from swing to rock as the day wears down resolve:
so hard it is to keep our notions tied

when the dark creeps in and our children dissolve
into motions we were always afraid
to make, whose forms we now stand in awe of.

This festival designed to celebrate
the bean and buck has gone too far astray:
Mennonites and Maconites, Iowegians of late,

Kansas Citians and Columbians pay
to grace our fairground with aluminum
cans and assorted cast-off crap. We say

each summer we'll stop the sale of condoms
and light beer inside the city limits,
but never make it law. We kept the bums,

however, well at bay: we gave no permits
for camping down by the tracks when the hobo king
suggested we coordinate times and sites,

put our festival and their conference thing
in one bin, as if to suggest the cost
were slight. They went on to Iowa, having

no other choice, long before the first frost.
Our crops grow smaller every year. We plant
and harvest with the almanac. Thus boast

we know what our fathers did, but we can't
seem to make our shrinking dollars equal
our bad debts. No matter how we may rant

and rave, one thing is sure: this festival
will stand as long as there are beans and banks.
Of what we've done, indeed it's best of all.

12. The Pastor's Farewell

FOR J. H.

To live here is to know the threat of storm
well enough to say it is no big deal
soybeans don't grow and our fields are foreign

landscapes to the eye. We tried too long to seal
our fates in silos packed with grain, to say
oh God, we're rich to the deliberating squeal

of sons we never knew would rule the day
the way we ruled the soil we took to till.
Friends, we are coming to a time we lay

our burdens on the closet shelf with will
and testament and want to go out clean,
and in that landscape of desire we fill

a grange hall with light laughter and, in
the center ring, the children we forever
want to be, all threat of storm within

our lives denied. Now the lovers' long star
burns out, now the river finds another shore,
now we become, now we end with what we are.

For the Suicide

The moon glides on water, the surface
black ice no one could walk on long
enough to count a heartbeat. Full,
dull moon that a gnat's eye could dim
or a lover's sigh could cause to slip
too soon into its darker sleep.

No one knows you are here, a risk
dared and done, your hands clean as stone
tumbled on the beach two hundred feet
below. Not one night bird cries, not
one wave sounds. The dark that touches
you consoles: your eyes write your name

on the offing you cannot see, nor
wish to see. You stand at the edge
of things—this cliff, tomorrow, your
life—and all the while not one song
for you to understand. To look
into the dark, you risk it all

and forever fail. Something triggers
need, and lovers fall. The ship sails
on, always toward the sunlit land.
The millionaire knocks on other doors.
You have no home inside your skin
that opens when the heart tides turn.

Deer Camp: Blue Mountain

At the western edge of the last ridge, you
wonder why the mountain stopped and refused
to turn the stream. The rutted road down ends
in the river bed. You make your camp in shadows
you no longer recognize. The way the water
charms you into yourself remains a mystery
constant as the sun. This was your larger
home when you were small. Now nothing is yours,
not even the deer, plentiful as ticks.

Two miles away the house you were born in
continues to buckle under the relentless
skies, though it never seems to lean toward
the river behind the barn. Sundown and you
hear ghosts of old dogs bark, two miles away
and ten thousand in curved time. The only
bridge across the river has recently
collapsed. The fences you remember have
disappeared into a forest of heavy pines.

You know why you came back, but cannot find
the words to put the wind right with this world,
the one world you had and lost. You're the kind
of fool that lets the deer browse in his camp.
Thank God for that. The only shot you'll take
is with a 35mm, and then only if the light
falls right. Those forty years seem a long shot.
From this angle of repose, you think it's
worth a try—to frame another kind of life.

From the Swinging Bridge

The shadows of bluegills seem
rapid arrows of light against
the vague algae and stones.

Swaying above the river
takes more breath than
good swimmers have to give.

Breathless in the rocking air,
you see your time flow
in the dark water
that will not stay
for shadows on the swinging bridge
nor ripples on the plane of sky
twenty feet below.

This parallel time behind
the deep water you look into
makes you want to step down
from the middle
and sink softly into
a dim semblance of self
that lives quite other.

But you cannot step
out of the swinging arc
of wind and your will
until the motion dies.

You walk across the water,
not into the dimmer sky below,
and feel the bridge
lift you upward with each step.

ACKNOWLEDGMENTS

On a Wing of the Sun

Many thanks to the Camargo Foundation (Cassis, France) and to Michael Pretina, the executive director, for the time and space to think and write.

The American Book of the Dead

Grateful acknowledgment is made to the National Endowment for the Arts for a writing fellowship that made the completion of many of these poems possible.

A portion of the section entitled "This Crazy Land" appeared in the chapbook *This Crazy Land* (Tempe, Arizona: Inland Boat Series/*Porch* Publications, 1980), copyright © 1980 by Jim Barnes.

The poems "Autobiography, Chapter 6: San Diego Harbor at Dusk," "Autobiography, Chapter 17: Floating the Big Piney," "Elegy for the Girl Who Drowned at Goats Bluff," "The Last Chance," "Midwest Midwinter" (under the title "Midwinter"), "Postcard to Grace Schulman" (under the title "Letter to a Poet"), and "Return to La Plata, Missouri," appeared in *The Nation*, copyright © 1975, 1976, 1977, 1978 by *The Nation*.

Grateful acknowledgment is made to the following publications in which many of the poems first appeared: *Chicago Review*: "The Body Falters," "Lost in Sulphur Canyons," "Pyramid Lake, Late Summer," and "Still-Hildreth Sanitarium: Ice Fishing" (under the title "Sanitarium Lake: Ice Fishing"); *Colorado North Review*: "For a Drowned Sailor, Age 4"; *CutBank*: "Autobiography, Chapter 4: The Mirage," "Autobiography, Chapter 9: Leaving, Again," and "Autobiography, Chapter 11: Prelude to Writing"; *Denver Quarterly*: "Autobiography, Chapter 12: Hearing Montana"; *Greenfield Review*: "Tornado"; *Green River Review*: "Swan Lake, Again"; *Images*: "On Top of Winding Stair Mountain"; *Invisible City*: "Autobiography, Chapter 1: Leaving Summerfield"; *Long Pond Review*: "Autobiographical Flashback: Puma and Pokeweed" and "On the Bridge at Fourche Maline River"; *Magic of Names*: "Autobiography, Chapter 16: Return to Rich Mountain"; *Mississippi Mud*: "Dog Days 1978" and "Loving the Distant Nude"; *Mississippi Valley Review*: "Contemporary Native American Poetry"; *Missouri Review*: "Memoirs of a Catskinner" and "My Father's House"; *El Nahuatzen*: "These Mysteries"; *The Nation*: "Autobiography, Chapter 6: San Diego Harbor at Dusk," "Autobiography, Chapter 17: Floating the Big Piney," "Elegy for the Girl Who Drowned at Goats Bluff," "The Last Chance," "Midwest Midwinter," "Postcard to Grace Schulman," and "Return to La Plata, Missouri"; *New America: A Review*: "Wild Horse Hollow"; *New Letters*: "Old Soldiers' Home at Marshalltown, Iowa"; *New Mexico Humanities Review*: "An Ex–Deputy Sheriff Remembers the Eastern Oklahoma Murderers"; *New*

River Review: "Stopping on Kiamichi Mountain"; *Northwest Review:* "Last Look at La Plata, Missouri"; *Outer Bridge:* "Autobiography, Chapter 13: Ghost Train, the Dream" and "The Only Photograph of Quentin at Harvard"; *Panache:* "Autobiography: Last Chapter"; *Phantasm:* "Autobiography, Chapter 2: Setting Out" and "Autobiography, Chapter 42: Three Days in Louisville"; *Poem:* "On the Beach at Manzanita, Oregon"; *Poetry Northwest:* "Against Metempsychosis &c." and "Scouting Tom Fry Hollow"; *Poetry Now:* "Under Buffalo Mountain"; *Practices of the Wind:* "Winter Pastoral"; *Quarry West:* "Autobiography, Chapter 7: Home for Memorial Day" and "The Exact Center of the World"; *Quarterly West:* "Autobiography, Chapter 14: Tombstone at Petit Bay, near Tahlequah," "Autobiography, Chapter 19: For Andrew Grossbardt, in Memoriam," and "San Miguel de Allende"; *Seattle Review:* "Comcomly's Skull"; *Separate Doors:* "On the Eve of My Parents' Sixtieth Anniversary"; *Shantih:* "The Chicago Odyssey" and "Year's End 1977"; *Slackwater Review:* "Autobiography, Chapter 8: At the Sand Fields" and "Sundown at Swan Lake, Missouri" (under the title "Sundown at Lake Tenkiller"); *South Dakota Review:* "Autobiography, Chapter 5: Ghost Town"; *Wanbli Ho:* "Tracking the Siuslaw Man"; *Wind:* "The Last Trip Somewhere West"; and *Wisconsin Review:* "In Rudolph's Cave."

A Season of Loss

Grateful acknowledgment is made to the following publications in which many of the poems first appeared: *Agni Review:* "Toy Soldiers"; *Arlington Quarterly:* "Dog Days"; *Beliot Poetry Journal:* "Near Crater Lake"; *Chicago Review:* "Notes for a Love Letter from Mid-America"; *Cimarron Review:* "5-Ring Circus at Season's End"; *Concerning Poetry:* "Halcyon Days"; *Coyote's Journal:* "Crow"; *CutBank:* "On the Mountain"; *Dacotah Territory:* "A Season of Loss"; *Georgia Review:* "Heartland"; *Green River Review:* "Call It Going with the Sun"; *Interstate:* "Badlands Mirage"; *Journal of Irish Literature:* "A Rannaigheacht Ghairid on Spring Burning"; *Kentucky Poetry Review:* "Parable"; *Laurel Review:* "The Long Lone Nevada Night Highway"; *Long Pond Review:* "At the Burn on the Oregon Coast"; *Mississippi Review:* "Sweating It Out on Winding Stair Mountain" and "Trying to Hide Out on Rich Mountain"; *The Nation:* "Four Things Choctaw" and "Postcard from Poison Spider Creek, Wyoming"; *New Letters:* "Accident at Three Mile Island" and "La Plata, Missouri: Clear November Night"; *Nimrod:* "Odyssey" and "Song of I-see-o"; *North Dakota Quarterly:* "Decades" and "Surviving the Storm"; *Pacific Quarterly Moana:* "A Season of Sun Dogs"; *Poem:* "A Song for All of Them" and "A Sunday Dreamer's Guide to Yarrow, Missouri"; *Poetry East:* "Dirge"; *Poetry Now:* "Yuma: The Greyhound Depot"; *The Point Riders Great Plains Poetry Anthology:* "January Wind"; *Prairie Schooner:* "Ghost Fog"; *Quartet:* "On Location at Tongue River"; *River Styx:* "Sundays"; *Rocky Mountain Review:* "Autobiography, Chapter 10: Circus in the Blood," "In Memory of a Day Nobody Remembers: September 26, 1874," and "The Sentence"; *Saltillo:* "Black Mesa Nocturn" and "Choctaw Cemetery"; *Seven:* "Bone Yard"; *Southern Poetry Review:* "Rest Stop at Horse Thief Spring"; *Southwest Review:* "Black Mesa Sundown"; *St. Andrews Review:* "The Captive Stone"; *Sunday Clothes:* "Rabbits" and "Right Place, Wrong Time"; *Texas Review:* "The Drowning"; *Three Rivers Poetry Journal:* "Return to the Roundup Tavern"; *Twigs:* "For Geoffrey

Firmin, in Hell"; and *West Coast Poetry Review:* "Paiute Ponies" and "Thunderstorm in a Nevada Ghost Town."

The following poems also appeared in *Carriers of the Dream Wheel: Contemporary Native American Poetry* (New York: Harper and Row, 1975): "Bone Yard," "The Captive Stone," "Halcyon Days," "Paiute Ponies," and "Sweating It Out on Winding Stair Mountain."

"A Sunday Dreamer's Guide to Yarrow, Missouri," also appeared in *Heartland 2: Poets of the Midwest* (Evanston: Northern Illinois University Press, 1975).

A word of gratitude and thanks is due to the National Endowment for the Arts; without the 1978 Fellowship in Poetry, this book would not have been completed.

La Plata Cantata

Many thanks are due Truman State University for a generous grant in the summer of 1987 that allowed me to cast this book in its final form. Many thanks are also due Neil Myers, professor of English at Purdue University, who made several helpful suggestions. In addition, grateful acknowledgment is made to the following publications in which many of the poems, some in slightly different versions, first appeared: *Amelia:* "Learning Balance"; *Bamboo Ridge:* "Night Letter to the Secretary of the Interior"; *Bloomsbury Review:* "Below the Sans Bois Mountain" and "Paraglyphs" (except the first section); *Boundary 2:* "Dreams the Children Had"; *Chariton Review:* "Trying to Read the Glyphs"; *Cincinnati Poetry Review:* "The Game"; *Confrontation:* "Behind the Lumberyard" and "Urn Burial"; *Denver Quarterly:* "Great Plains Tornado"; *The First Skin around Me: Contemporary American Tribal Poetry:* "The Submarine in the Park between the Muskogee Toll Road and the Arkansas River"; *Green River Review:* "Surveying near Ellsworth, Kansas" (under the title "Two Poems on One Theme"); *Hayden's Ferry Review:* "Going after the Milch Cow" and "Souvenirs"; *Interstate:* "Stations" (under the title "Pumps"); *Kansas Quarterly:* "Ubi Sunt"; *Kenyon Review:* "Bandstand" and "The Santa Fe Depot" (under the title "Santa Fe Depot, Sundown"); *Laurel Review:* "Crossing the Kiamichis Again," "For the Suicide," and "The War over Holson Valley"; *Long Pond Review:* "At 39: The View from Sycamore Tower"; *Missouri Review:* "Gill Netting the Beaver Pond"; *The Nation:* "Domain"; *New Collage:* "In Hugo Country"; *New Letters:* "Circus Poster," "Icons," "Memories of Oceanside," and "Once in Winnemucca"; *Nimrod:* "Postcard from Blue Finger Lake"; *Ohio Review:* "Turkey Season"; *Paintbrush:* "Heavy Metal," "The Light above the Store," "The Palace Cafe," and "Savage Country"; *Phoenix:* "Near Cimarron, New Mexico"; *Poem:* "The Heavener Runes" (under the title "Rune"); *Poetry Northwest:* "Touching the Rattlesnake"; *Poetry Wales:* "The Pastor's Farewell"; *Quarterly West:* "Bombardier"; *River Styx:* "Deer Camp: Blue Mountain"; *Sulphur River:* the first section of "Paraglyphs" (under the title "Petroglyphs"); *West Coast Poetry Review:* "Something in the Blood"; *Winewood Journal:* "South Willamette Valley Bars: A Memoir"; and *Zone 3:* "Hunting Winding Stair Mountain."

The poems "Domain," "The Submarine in the Park between the Muskogee Toll Road and the Arkansas River," and "Trying to Read the Glyphs" also appeared in a limited edition volume, *The Fish on Poteau Mountain* (Stillwater, Okla.: Cedar Creek Press, 1980), copyright 1980 by Jim Barnes.

Jim Barnes has published eight volumes of poetry, including *Paris* and *The Sawdust War*, and two volumes of poetry in translation. His many honors include a National Endowment for the Arts fellowship, the Pushcart Prize, a Rockefeller Foundation fellowship, a Fulbright fellowship, and two Camargo Foundation fellowships. His autobiography, *On Native Ground: Memoirs and Impressions*, won the American Book Award. He is currently writer-in-residence and professor of comparative literature at Truman State University.

Illinois Poetry Series
Laurence Lieberman, Editor

History Is Your Own Heartbeat
Michael S. Harper (1971)

The Foreclosure
Richard Emil Braun (1972)

The Scrawny Sonnets and Other Narratives
Robert Bagg (1973)

The Creation Frame
Phyllis Thompson (1973)

To All Appearances: Poems New and Selected
Josephine Miles (1974)

The Black Hawk Songs
Michael Borich (1975)

Nightmare Begins Responsibility
Michael S. Harper (1975)

The Wichita Poems
Michael Van Walleghen (1975)

Images of Kin: New and Selected Poems
Michael S. Harper (1977)

Poems of the Two Worlds
Frederick Morgan (1977)

Cumberland Station
Dave Smith (1977)

Tracking
Virginia R. Terris (1977)

Riversongs
Michael Anania (1978)

On Earth as It Is
Dan Masterson (1978)

Coming to Terms
Josephine Miles (1979)

Death Mother and Other Poems
Frederick Morgan (1979)

Goshawk, Antelope
Dave Smith (1979)

Local Men
James Whitehead (1979)

Searching the Drowned Man
Sydney Lea (1980)

With Akhmatova at the Black Gates
Stephen Berg (1981)

Dream Flights
Dave Smith (1981)

More Trouble with the Obvious
Michael Van Walleghen (1981)

The American Book of the Dead
Jim Barnes (1982)

The Floating Candles
Sydney Lea (1982)

Northbook
Frederick Morgan (1982)

Collected Poems, 1930–83
Josephine Miles (1983; reissue, 1999)

The River Painter
Emily Grosholz (1984)

Healing Song for the Inner Ear
Michael S. Harper (1984)

The Passion of the Right-Angled Man
T. R. Hummer (1984)

Dear John, Dear Coltrane
Michael S. Harper (1985)

Poems from the Sangamon
John Knoepfle (1985)

In It
Stephen Berg (1986)

The Ghosts of Who We Were
Phyllis Thompson (1986)

Moon in a Mason Jar
Robert Wrigley (1986)

Lower-Class Heresy
T. R. Hummer (1987)

Poems: New and Selected
Frederick Morgan (1987)

Furnace Harbor: A Rhapsody of the North Country
Philip D. Church (1988)

Bad Girl, with Hawk
Nance Van Winckel (1988)

Blue Tango
Michael Van Walleghen (1989)

Eden
Dennis Schmitz (1989)

Waiting for Poppa at the Smithtown Diner
Peter Serchuk (1990)

Great Blue
Brendan Galvin (1990)

What My Father Believed
Robert Wrigley (1991)

Something Grazes Our Hair
S. J. Marks (1991)

Walking the Blind Dog
G. E. Murray (1992)

The Sawdust War
Jim Barnes (1992)

The God of Indeterminacy
Sandra McPherson (1993)

Off-Season at the Edge of the World
Debora Greger (1994)

Counting the Black Angels
Len Roberts (1994)

Oblivion
Stephen Berg (1995)

To Us, All Flowers Are Roses
Lorna Goodison (1995)

Honorable Amendments
Michael S. Harper (1995)

Points of Departure
Miller Williams (1995)

Dance Script with Electric Ballerina
Alice Fulton (reissue, 1996)

To the Bone: New and Selected Poems
Sydney Lea (1996)

Floating on Solitude
Dave Smith (3-volume reissue, 1996)

Bruised Paradise
Kevin Stein (1996)

Walt Whitman Bathing
David Wagoner (1996)

Rough Cut
Thomas Swiss (1997)

Paris
Jim Barnes (1997)

The Ways We Touch
Miller Williams (1997)

The Rooster Mask
Henry Hart (1998)

The Trouble-Making Finch
Len Roberts (1998)

Grazing
Ira Sadoff (1998)

Turn Thanks
Lorna Goodison (1999)

Traveling Light:
Collected and New Poems
David Wagoner (1999)

Some Jazz a While:
Collected Poems
Miller Williams (1999)

The Iron City
John Bensko (2000)

Songlines in Michaeltree: New and
Collected Poems
Michael S. Harper (2000)

Pursuit of a Wound
Sydney Lea (2000)

The Pebble: Old and New Poems
Mairi MacInnes (2000)

Chance Ransom
Kevin Stein (2000)

House of Poured-Out Waters
Jane Mead (2001)

The Silent Singer: New and Selected
Poems
Len Roberts (2001)

The Salt Hour
J. P. White (2001)

National Poetry Series

Eroding Witness
Nathaniel Mackey (1985)
Selected by Michael S. Harper

Palladium
Alice Fulton (1986)
Selected by Mark Strand

Cities in Motion
Sylvia Moss (1987)
Selected by Derek Walcott

The Hand of God and a Few
Bright Flowers
William Olsen (1988)
Selected by David Wagoner

The Great Bird of Love
Paul Zimmer (1989)
Selected by William Stafford

Stubborn
Roland Flint (1990)
Selected by Dave Smith

The Surface
Laura Mullen (1991)
Selected by C. K. Williams

The Dig
Lynn Emanuel (1992)
Selected by Gerald Stern

My Alexandria
Mark Doty (1993)
Selected by Philip Levine

The High Road to Taos
Martin Edmunds (1994)
Selected by Donald Hall

Theater of Animals
Samn Stockwell (1995)
Selected by Louise Glück

The Broken World
Marcus Cafagña (1996)
Selected by Yusef Komunyakaa

Nine Skies
A. V. Christie (1997)
Selected by Sandra McPherson

Lost Wax
Heather Ramsdell (1998)
Selected by James Tate

So Often the Pitcher Goes to Water until It Breaks
Rigoberto González (1999)
Selected by Ai

Renunciation
Corey Marks (2000)
Selected by Philip Levine

Manderley
Rebecca Wolff (2001)
Selected by Robert Pinsky

Other Poetry Volumes

Local Men and *Domains*
James Whitehead (1987)

Her Soul beneath the Bone: Women's Poetry on Breast Cancer
Edited by Leatrice Lifshitz (1988)

Days from a Dream Almanac
Dennis Tedlock (1990)

Working Classics: Poems on Industrial Life
Edited by Peter Oresick and Nicholas Coles (1990)

Hummers, Knucklers, and Slow Curves: Contemporary Baseball Poems
Edited by Don Johnson (1991)

The Double Reckoning of Christopher Columbus
Barbara Helfgott Hyett (1992)

Selected Poems
Jean Garrigue (1992)

New and Selected Poems, 1962–92
Laurence Lieberman (1993)

The Dig and *Hotel Fiesta*
Lynn Emanuel (1994)

For a Living: The Poetry of Work
Edited by Nicholas Coles and Peter Oresick (1995)

The Tracks We Leave: Poems on Endangered Wildlife of North America
Barbara Helfgott Hyett (1996)

Peasants Wake for Fellini's *Casanova* and Other Poems
Andrea Zanzotto; edited and translated by John P. Welle and Ruth Feldman; drawings by Federico Fellini and Augusto Murer (1997)

Moon in a Mason Jar and *What My Father Believed*
Robert Wrigley (1997)

The Wild Card: Selected Poems, Early and Late
Karl Shapiro; edited by Stanley Kunitz and David Ignatow (1998)

Turtle, Swan and *Bethlehem in Broad Daylight*
Mark Doty (2000)

Illinois Voices: An Anthology of Twentieth-Century Poetry
Edited by Kevin Stein and G. E. Murray (2001)

On a Wing of the Sun
Jim Barnes (3-volume reissue, 2001)

The University of Illinois Press
is a founding member of the
Association of American University Presses.

Composed in 10/13 Electra LH
with Electra LH display
by Jim Proefrock
at the University of Illinois Press
Designed by Paula Newcomb
Manufactured by Cushing-Malloy, Inc.

University of Illinois Press
1325 South Oak Street
Champaign, IL 61820-6903
www.press.uillinois.edu